NEWCASTLE/BLOODAXE POETRY SERIES: 5

CAROL RUMENS:

SELF INTO SONG

NEWCASTLE/BLOODAXE POETRY SERIES

1: Linda Anderson & Jo Shapcott (eds.)
Elizabeth Bishop: Poet of the Periphery

2: David Constantine: *A Living Language:*
NEWCASTLE / BLOODAXE POETRY LECTURES

3: Julia Darling & Cynthia Fuller (eds.)
The Poetry Cure

4: Jo Shapcott: *The Transformers:*
NEWCASTLE / BLOODAXE POETRY LECTURES
[Delayed title: now due 2008]

5: Carol Rumens: *Self into Song:*
NEWCASTLE / BLOODAXE POETRY LECTURES

6: Desmond Graham: *Making Poems and Their Meanings:*
NEWCASTLE / BLOODAXE POETRY LECTURES

NEWCASTLE/BLOODAXE POETRY LECTURES

In this innovative series of public lectures at the University of Newcastle upon Tyne, leading contemporary poets speak about the craft and practice of poetry to audiences drawn from both the city and the university. The lectures are then published in book form by Bloodaxe, giving readers everywhere the opportunity to learn what the poets themselves think about their own subject.

NEWCASTLE/BLOODAXE POETRY SERIES: 5

CAROL RUMENS

Self into Song

NEWCASTLE / BLOODAXE POETRY LECTURES

BLOODAXE BOOKS

Copyright © Carol Rumens 2004, 2007

ISBN: 978 1 85224 760 7

First published 2007 by
Department of English Literary & Linguistic Studies,
University of Newcastle,
Newcastle upon Tyne NE1 7RU,
in association with
Bloodaxe Books Ltd,
Highgreen,
Tarset,
Northumberland NE48 1RP.

www.bloodaxebooks.com
For further information about Bloodaxe titles
please visit our website or write to
the above address for a catalogue.

Bloodaxe Books Ltd acknowledges
the financial assistance of
Arts Council England, North East.

Cover design: Neil Astley & Pamela Robertson-Pearce.

Cover printing: J. Thomson Colour Printers Ltd, Glasgow.

Printed in Great Britain by
Bell & Bain Limited, Glasgow, Scotland.

Contents

Acknowledgements

Many thanks to Bloodaxe Books and to the University of Newcastle upon Tyne for inviting me to participate in their lecture series, particularly Neil Astley, Desmond Graham, Linda Anderson and Bill Herbert. Thanks also to Patricia McCarthy, editor of *Agenda*, for commissioning a review of Derek Mahon's *Collected Poems* for the triple Irish Issue (Vol.40, Nos. 1-3), in which some of the ideas contained in 'Far from the Venal Roar' first took shape.

I am indebted to the University of Hull, and particularly to George Talbot, Dean of the Faculty of Arts and Social Sciences, for the period of study-leave which enabled me to work on these three pieces. I am also grateful to the University of Wales, Bangor, for generously extending that leave.

To Becky, true scholar and inspiring daughter, and to Yura, enduringly patient, love and thanks beyond words.

I 'Far from the Venal Roar?': Isolation and Conversation in the Poetry of Derek Mahon

Derek Mahon's work brings to mind the phrase, 'nostalgia for world culture', Osip Mandelstam's well-known aphoristic definition of the Russian poetic movement, Acmeism. Mahon is almost a one-man Acemist Movement, devoted to traditional norms and forms of excellence (*akme* is the Greek word for excellence) and searching restlessly to discover such forms in past and other cultures. In doing so he creates a community of like minds as a kind of contraflow to more restrictive local communities.

Art for Mahon has appeared sometimes to demand a certain rage *against* order, if not the 'long, immense and systematic disorder of the senses' advised by Rimbaud. This is a matter of the life and the work, and particularly the way the poetry is employed to construct the life – which appears to involve sacrificial solitude as well as comradely Bohemianism. Politics of course impinges. But, to put it crudely, Northern Ireland's Troubles for such an artist are only part of the trouble: the *poète maudit* walks in other shadows. One shadow attaches to the attraction/repulsion conflict about society, expressed in the 5th section of the sequence, 'Light Music':

> I built my house
> in a forest far
> from the venal roar.
>
> Somebody please
> beat a path
> to my door.
>
> ('Please')[1]

Born to a working-class Protestant family in County Antrim in 1941, educated via Trinity College, Dublin, where he read French and English, Mahon to some extent typifies the 'learning-curve' of a generation of Northern Irish poets who emerged

7

from ethnically determined backgrounds and were liberated by education to explore wider political and literary landscapes. Translation seems to have been part of that anti-sectarian, anti-parochial project. Seamus Heaney's career as a translator has been equally distinguished and almost as wide-ranging (it includes Dante, Sophocles, the Beowulf poet): Michael Longley has made a significant part of his life's work the imaginative transformation of Homer and Ovid. By temperament and profession a freelance, Mahon literarily uprooted his imagination at an early stage of his career, spending a year in France at the Sorbonne after he left Trinity, then moving on to Canada, the USA and England. Typically, he has 'divided his time' between New York, London and the Republic of Ireland, currently West Cork. His translations include plays by Euripides, Racine, Molière and Cyrano de Bergerac. A properly full study of his original poetry would examine how it has assimilated the writers he has so empathetically translated, particularly the poets Gérard de Nerval and Philippe Jaccottet.

Mahon's immediate mentors range from the formal masters W.B. Yeats and Louis MacNeice to the Modernists James Joyce and Samuel Beckett. It is to the latter he owes a key concept, 'the existential lyric'. Reviewing the *Collected Poems in English and French*, he links the phrase with Beckett's sense of metaphysical 'rupture' and need to escape from 'tongue-tied profanity' (which) 'has less to do with economic conditions than with, in Pascal's phrase, 'la misère de l'homme sans dieu'.[2] Mahon's own work is imbued with a similar sense of radical exile.

This work is receptive to a range of philosophical ideas. Broadly, it enacts the existentialist position as defined by Sartre: 'The attempt to draw all the consequences from a position of consistent atheism' (Philip Larkin's position was similar). This does not mean that either poet operates in a vacuum bare of any system. Mahon's work proposes organic continuity, invoking the ancient philosopher-scientists whose atomism so extraordinarily anticipates current understanding – Heraclitus, with his concept of existence as perpetual flux, and Lucretius, embryonic evolutionist.[3] Flirting with notions of metempsychosis, he peoples the world with sub-atomic or semi-human, though ever-transient, forms of consciousness. It often seems that he agrees with Pythagoras that 'everything is susceptible'.[4] Souls transmigrate into things, things stare back at the starer. In 'The Studio' [5] the restrained disturbance of objects and fixtures blends with the disturbance of the (significantly absent) artist's portraits: 'Its mourning faces are cracked porcelain only quicker, / its knuckles doorknobs only lighter, / its occasional cries of despair / a function of the furniture'. His animism is characteristically benign and seems to relate to the experiences of an only child, for whom the material world, friendly or indifferent, is often his sole society. His tenderest, perhaps most tragic, portrait of Northern Ireland filters the focus through an entropy of household objects:

> The chair squeaks in a high wind,
> Rain falls from its branches;
> The kettle years for the mountain,
> The soap for the sea.
> In a tiny stone church
> On a desolate headland
> A lost tribe is singing 'Abide with Me'. [6]

The 'lost tribe', intoning its great, impassioned Protestant hymn to a contested, probably non-existent deity, has of course, no final originary destination in which to be absorbed, apart from the air – the fourth unspoken element if earth here is represented by the tree, fire by the mountain and water by the sea. The last two lines could be read as a prediction of the demise of Unionism, but that would sell short the ontological quality of the vision. This marvellous little "existential lyric" expresses a loss that for Mahon is central to the human condition.

Residual theism is glimpsed perhaps in Mahon's contrary attraction to a stilled, Zen-like poetics of the image, as in parts of 'Light Music'. [7] His moments of moral self-criticism suggest there are ethical as well as aesthetic absolutes, connected ultimately to the sense of an interrogation by a vigilant eternity – not God, of course, but perhaps MacNeice's alternative, as in 'God – or whatever means the good'.

It was at his grammar school, the Royal Belfast Academical Institution, that Mahon met the poet who would become his closest literary friend. Michael Longley was two years his senior. 'I first viewed him guiltily out of the corner of my eye in the school library,' Longley recollects. 'I felt guilty because the

Muse had already brushed me lightly with her wing when I was sixteen, but I had ignored the invitation and allowed that side of myself to go underground. An aesthete in private, a hearty in public...I followed my friends in smirking knowingly when Mahon was pointed out: "Thinks he's a poet".' [8]

Mahon probably thought right. All we know of his early work is polished, fluent and sophisticated. There is no awkward 'digging' for roots, no muddied search for the 'personal Helicon' that bothered and energised the young Heaney. His earliest influences seem to have been the poetry of Yeats, transmuted by a memorable literature teacher originally from Dublin, John Boyle, and the rhythms and rhetoric of the Church of Ireland hymns (Mahon was a choir-boy). In an interview with John Brown the poet recalls the line by Isaac Watts, 'Ransomed, healed, restored, forgiven', as a proof of how 'the hymnology invaded the mind'.[9] Both sources help account for the strong formal underpinnings of his poetry.

The two young Belfast poets properly made contact at TCD. Longley, an editor of the college magazine, *Icarus*, accepted for publication a poem by Mahon called 'Subsidy Bungalows'. This poem remains uncollected, but Longley's description suggests it was an early version of the poem 'Glengormley' which appeared in Mahon's first collection, *Night Crossing*, published in 1968, when he was 27. It begins:

> Wonders are many and none is more wonderful than man
> Who has tamed the terrier, trimmed the hedge
> And grasped the principle of the watering-can.
> Clothes-pegs litter the window-ledge
> And the long ships lie in clover; washing lines
> Shake out white linen over the chalk thanes.[10]

Mahon has arrived already at his most characteristic 'angle' – the wry stare at a place that is physically home, but intellectually alien. The most striking feature of the poem is perhaps its emotional maturity. The quotation from Sophocles that forms the first line is brilliantly tilted into bathos in lines 2 and 3, but mockery doesn't turn out to be the poem's goal. Mahon resists his own cleverness. As the stanzas unfold, it's as if the speaker is striving to observe his suburban community through a lens more complex than youthful scorn. Like 'Courtyards in

Delft' [11] which it foreshadows, the poem creates an edgy balance of antithetical images and emotions. In stanza 2, Ulster's mythical monsters and Cuchulainn-like 'giants / Who tore up sods twelve miles by six / And hurled them out to sea to become islands' are impotent. They are replaced by heroic human figures who, though they no longer 'bring dangerous tokens to the new era' are not so dispensable. 'Their sad names linger in the histories'. These vaguely imagined characters, Irish and/or possibly French revolutionary activists, have failed and been punished by execution or suicide. They form, with the suffering artist, a community of 'The unreconciled in their metaphysical pain' (we remember Beckett's sense of 'rupture' as decoded by Mahon) whose bodies, dangling from lamp-posts, are revealed by the light of a wet dawn. But the final stanza sees a further shift of focus, as the speaker supposes that the tragic activists had 'pictured' just such a banal suburb as they 'struggled through / the quick noose of their finite being'. The verb 'pictured' surely hints that the calm life of the suburb was not simply seen: it was remembered and reinvented in death as a beloved home.

The poem's speaker, too, sees beyond the bourgeois trappings to a more transcendental sense of order. Home becomes visionary in the wonderfully-evoked light and cleanliness (as well as ahistorical flatness) of the local scenery: 'the long ships lie in clover; washing lines / Shake out white linen over the chalk thanes'. Echoing, then revising, the words of the hymnal, the speaker exhorts himself to 'praise' the 'worldly'. The final submission, a wittily grave moral memo-to-self is typical: '...by / Necessity if not choice I live here too'. But of course it is the cast of the disaffected that has appeared at the most climactic point in the poem. The Dante-esque image of the corpses haunts the last stanza's reprise of 'The terrier-taming, garden-watering days'... The phrase 'metaphysical pain' has betrayed the speaker's empathy with these figures. To the end, the poem sustains its emotional balancing act. But however even-handed the evaluation, however solid the assertion 'I live here too', the deeper impression remains that it is not by choice that the speaker would be located there.

'You might say that my first model of community was tainted, so I opted out of community,' Mahon told John Brown in the interview quoted above. The taint may include a sectarian one, but simple narrow-minded repression is also adverted to. An only childhood in a household where the father worked long hours and the mother devoted all her energies to housework, might remind us of Larkin's English midlands background.[12] Sectarian violence came later and sealed the abyss. 'I felt very far from home in these years...In fact, a large part of my life I've been *terrified* of home' Mahon confesses. 'I was horrified and didn't go up there after a certain point'.[13]

Because in maturity each would evolve a highly distinct poetic manner, it is easy to overlook some areas of similarity in early work by Longley and Mahon. Diction is an example. The lexicon of both writers tends to favour words of Latin origin, and at times they adopt a Latin-influenced syntax, allowing for a degree of hyper-baton unusual among young poets in the 1960s. (Yeats, of course, also exerts an influence here.) The sentence may begin with a subordinate clause, as, for example, in Mahon's 'Canadian Pacific': 'From famine, pestilence and persecution / those gaunt forefathers shipped abroad to find / rough stone of heaven beyond the western ocean / and staked their claim, and pinned their faith'.[14] The first stanza of Michael Longley's 'The Hebrides' (see below) is similarly structured. The more patrician tone and hieratic sense of cadence are, interestingly, to be found in early Longley. Later, the situation concerning tone is somewhat reversed: Mahon continues to adopt a vatic air where he sees fit, while Longley, without loss of fastidiousness, eases down to a more gently demotic pitch.

Both poets at times make use of an unusual stanzaic device of stepped lineation derived from George Herbert. Each accentual syllabic stanza is composed of lines variously indented, sometimes but not always reflecting their metrical length. It is a layout that pleases the eye with its symmetry, and the ear with its enhancement of melody and cadence. Variants of the device occur in Longley's poems 'Epithalamium', 'The Hebrides', and 'A Personal Statement'. It also appears, rather later, in Mahon's 'The Banished Gods', 'The Hunt by Night' and 'Girls on the Bridge'.

In whom the city is continuing
I stop to look,
To find my feet among the ling
And bracken – over me
The bright continuum of gulls, a rook
Occasionally.

(Longley: 'The Hebrides')[15]

Paros, far-shining star of dark-blue earth,
Reverts to the sea its mother.
The tiny particles,
Rose, quartz and amethyst,
Panic into the warm brine together.

(Mahon: 'The Banished Gods')[16]

Longley reveals the good-humoured 'jousting' from which such variations on a theme of Herbert evolved:

'Epithalamium' is the first poem of mine to survive. I wrote it in the summer of 1963 when I should have been studying for my finals. The stanza-shape is Herbert-like, but my own invention. Derek Mahon had sent me a poem written along similar lines, so I knocked together an even more taxing stanzaic pattern and rhyme-scheme and let my sentences unwind through many stanzas – a 1500 metres race, only with hurdles. I wrote 'Epithalamium' in an elated rush, despite the formal difficulties…I was jousting with Mahon and with George Herbert'.[17]

We must assume, between the lines, that Mahon, who'd clearly initiated the 'joust' was, in his reticent way, jousting back.

Mahon's invocation of his true imaginative 'people' begins with the valediction to Louis MacNeice, 'In Carrowdore Churchyard'.[18] The poem is both elegy and panegyric. Moving with beautiful ease between high style and demotic, it praises vulnerability as well as rigor as aspects of the creative life. Rimbaud, de Nerval, Van Gogh, de Quincey, Malcolm Lowry will be added to the pantheon – artists who suffered both 'metaphysical' and (sometimes self-induced) physical pain but whose art attained wholeness and perhaps justified their disordered lives. These figures are engaged with intimately, as subjects of poems or translation. In entering their imaginative worlds, or summoning their presences, it's as if Mahon recruits his own Bohemian army. Beckett's Molloy, a kind of alter ego, is there, too. They do not as much keep at bay as allow him an imaginative angle on the dismal facts – the brutality and bigotry of the Troubles, provincial small-mindedness, the various 'benighted' coasts of exile,[19] the cold wind of nihilism and the productive/destructive trajectories of alcohol addiction.

However, he remains earthed by 'worldly' friends and contemporaries. In the first three books alone there are poems for the following: Jill Schlesinger, Colin Middleton, Edna Longley, Eamon Grennan, Tom and Peggy McIntyre, 'Doreen' (Mahon's wife), Bill McCormack, Seamus Heaney, Jeremy Lewis, James Simmons, Louis Asekoff, J.G. Farrell, Maurice Leitch, John Hewitt and Michael Longley. It is this social dimension which perhaps guarantees against the portentousness that might easily ensue from his tragic vision. Mahon's work avoids self-pity. There are invariably undertones of irony and/or self-mockery, and a frequent bracing intellectual detachment. As the discipline of the metrical line permits the expression of emotion, so the sense of audience provides the self-awareness that lends wit and detachment to the tone.

It is not the simple polarity of wretched home *versus* ideal homelessness that renders Mahon a poet of divided affiliations. His rejection of his originating community (a moral as well as artistic rejection) is a matter for his conscience, which then harasses him against his chosen displacement. In the early poem 'The Spring Vacation', later re-titled 'Spring in Belfast',[20] self-chastisement seems to reach a crisis:

> One part of my mind must learn to know its place.
> The things that happen in the kitchen houses
> And echoing back streets of this desperate city
> Should engage more than my casual interest,
> Exact more interest than my casual pity.

The tone here is less self-accommodating than that of 'Rather, I should praise...' The location is significant: this is warring Belfast, not pre-Troubles Glengormley. The cost of disengagement has been raised. Despite the fact that it is positioned first in the *Collected Poems*, it must have been written, or completed, considerably later than 'Glengormley'. Belfast was not yet such a 'desperate city' in 1964. Similarly, in Part 2 of 'Afterlives', Mahon, '...going home by sea / For the first time in years' admonishes himself for a failure of loyalty that he fears is also a failure of poetic maturity: 'Perhaps if I'd stayed behind / And lived it bomb by bomb / I might have grown up at last / And learnt what is meant by home.' [21]

'Rage for Order' [22] confronts this guilt head-on. The 'Glengormley' revolutionaries are welded into a single terrorist-speaker in an extraordinarily self-scourging, consistently oxymoronic monologue. The protagonist is permitted to denounce poetry with a poet's full rhetorical eloquence and moral authority. He, too, sees himself as a kind of artist, and subject to artistic theatricality and anxiety as he commands the real poet, now an ineffectual onlooker, to 'Watch as I tear down / To build up/ with a desperate love'. For a moment, as he passes judgement against the poet in contemporary society ('He is far / From his people'), he seems to speak with a terrible wisdom.

'Know your place' is a familiar put-down, revealing the backbone of provincial working-class etiquette and ethics. Heaney famously worried about his place in a Catholic farming community because his 'digging' would have to be accomplished by pen instead of spade.[23] In embattled communities the bonds of family and tribal loyalty grip still tighter. Location, which, at its crudest level, denotes religion and associated ethnicity, is of course aesthetically crucial. Northern poets construct place as poetic personality, giving access to a distinct topography and idiolect.

Writing about home enabled Northern Catholic poets to own their unhomely territory. Heaney began with his Derry roots, then looked South for their originating ground. Ciaran Carson, more recently, has mapped the Belfast pavements his father trod as a postman, a neighbourhood once threatened by raids and bombs and now by redevelopment.[24] For Protestants of a similar generation, supporting Catholic emancipation but rooted in societies whose political attitudes were more likely to be defensive, there would be a particular creative challenge. Both Mahon, peripatetic, and Longley, settled in Belfast, build in their work alternative aesthetic homes. Mahon is not so much an inner émigré, though, as an inner resident; in his early career he is outside looking back, and grapples constantly with the problem of despondent return, almost as if the process were the place.

The ambivalence may register at the level of voice. 'Home-coming'[25] begins colloquially, recalling the six-hour flight from Boston to Dublin: 'drunk all night / with crashing bore / from Houston, Tex. / who spoke at length/ of guns and sex'. The 'crashing bore' himself wouldn't have any difficulty so far. But, as the narrative progresses, the tone slides up a few notches: 'skies change but not / souls change; behold / this is the way / the world grows old'. Even allowing for a tinge of characteristic irony in the hymnal hyperbole of 'behold!', there is enough intensity here (note the Latinate negative construction, 'not souls change') to indicate that Mahon has changed vocal gear. In Ireland it seems there is easier access to poetic, even bardic diction ('skies', 'souls', 'behold') and lament.

The Northern rant of 'Ecclesiastes'[26] has an entirely different pace. The speaker, now on home ground, pours maledictions on the life-negating Sunday scene, the religion of non-forgiveness and denial. But the anger is partly whipped up because he cannot quite hate the place enough, despite all his principles and predilections:

> God, you could grow to love it, God-fearing, God-
> chosen purist little puritan that,
> for all your wiles and smiles, you are (the
> dank churches, the empty streets,
> the shipyard silences, the tied-up swings) and
> shelter your cold heart from the heat
> of the world, from woman-inquisition, from the
> bright eyes of children...

The verse is fluid, yet has none of the psalm-like plangency of the original Ecclesiastes. Its staccato line-breaks seem to gasp for air. It enacts expression and repression simultaneously in an extraordinary, choked riff that finally strangles, as it proclaims, the speaker's intention to suppress the flâneur in himself, to 'Bury that red / bandana and stick, that banjo' and 'stand on a corner stiff / with rhetoric, promising nothing under the sun'. Both 'Ecclesiastes' and 'I am Raftery'[27] show Mahon experimenting with mis-match of line and syntax, combining the free-falling enjambement of the stress-limited, colloquial kind of poem with vigorous accentuation. 'Ecclesiastes' is the more skilfully controlled, a contest of powerful equals. The poem is metrically an iron-ribbed cage that buckles as it is attacked by the bird of damnation and free verse. It's as if Ian Paisley and William Carlos Williams were battling it out in the same pulpit.

Writing letters home or from home gives the ambivalent loner the best of several worlds: company, but at a safe distance, a double imaginative location. Mahon's troubled sociability expresses itself in epistolary poems more often soliloquy than implied dialogue. They occasionally invoke a 'we', rarely a 'you'. 'Beyond Howth Head', dedicated to Jeremy Lewis, is one of the exceptions, even going so far as to use the addressee's first name in the poem's text.[28] While his network extends beyond poets and northerners, his own generation of Ulster poets remains crucial. These poets, separated by adult careers and loyalties, still know each other intimately as critics, comrades, rivals. They respond acutely to each other's work. Within the broader social picture, poetry draws on a particularly verbal and communicative tradition. *Craic* figures large in Irish social life, North and South, and poetry in Ireland, as in Wales, retains some of its bardic characteristics as a sociable, even publicly accountable, art form. A poem may have a single addressee, or none, but it is hardly a private communication. The northern writers want to be heard and over-heard in poetry's *agora*.

Mahon's dedicated poems can, however, seem intimate, as if they permitted the writer a confessional unmasking, a friendly but unanswering context in which to expose opinions and emotions and, of course, that opinionated emotion, guilt. 'Thinking of Inis Oirr in Cambridge, Mass'[29] is a wonderful little *paysage moralise* offering its 'dream of limestone in sea-light' to the Southern poet Eamon Grennan. Even here, home casts a shadow:

Atlantic leagues away tonight,
Conceived beyond such innocence,
I clutch the memory still, and I
Have measured everything with it since.   (*My italics.*)

Poetry's ideal landscape is un-peopled: compare the image of 'tainted community' with the elemental 'innocence' of the un-contested, sparsely-populated island. While the maturing imagination may be better-fed by a *dérive* around the globe than a dig in Glengormley, its true place seems to be in absolute solitude

17

on the edge of the sea. Community for Mahon seems by its very nature to be tainted.

Formally, all kinds of participants contribute to the poetic conversation. For example, the melodious, antiphonally structured 'Afterlives' is dedicated to James Simmons – another Northern poet who wrote, in addition, music and lyrics, and who was an exponent of the light vernacular style. Both the trimetric rhythm and the tone may remind us of Auden's choice for his 1939 'New Year Letter': 'I sit in one of the dives / On Fifty-second Street'.[30] There is a similar first-person present-tense scene-setting for each section: 'I wake in a dark flat', 'I am going home by sea'. The fifth stanza brings an echo of the Larkin classic mix of tone-lowering demotic and resonant symbol: 'What middle-class shits we are / to imagine for one second / That our privileged ideals / Are divine wisdom, and the dim / forms that kneel at noon / In the city not ourselves'. 'Shits' in the later collections replaces the original 'cunts', and the marginally muted insult, whether applied for literary reasons or to correct "sexist" language, furnishes a smoother and perhaps more linguistically connected sentence – note the 'privy' in 'privileged'. Instances of internal rhyme ('the places I grew up in / the faces that try to explain') recall Louis MacNeice's 'The Sunlight on the Garden': 'The sunlight on the garden / Hardens and grows cold'.[31] And we shouldn't forget Robert Burns, whose characteristic verse-letter tone so perfectly demonstrates the jauntiness of spirit, even in adversity, demanded by a sociable art-form.

The exchanges between the Northern poets may encode acts of literary criticism. In 'Lives', for example, Mahon seems to target the archaeological-ideological construct that Seamus Heaney had embarked on in *Wintering Out*, and which would culminate in the subsequent volume *North*. Heaney tends to elide historical and political eras. He may almost romantically identify with his Bronze Age ancestors, see 'Tinder' and even the fine-tuned and reticent 'The Tollund Man'[32] Mahon's playful *reductio* is voiced by a time-travelling bunch of atoms, constantly changing role: 'First time out / I was a torc of gold / And wept tears of the sun. // That was fun / But they buried me / In the earth two thousand years / Till a labourer / Turned me up with a pick / In eighteen forty-four // And sold me / For tea and sugar / In Newmarket-on-Fergus'.[33] This artefact-ancestor seems to be saying, along with Heraclitus, that everything is flux, and that there may be an arrogance as well as anachronism in setting up historical parallels: 'And if in the distant / Future someone / Thinks he has been me / As I am today // Let him revise / His insolent ontology / Or teach himself to pray' This is a poem *for* Heaney, not *to* him: that is, it's a gift. Wrapping up a seemingly barbed criticism, the poem asks not to be given the dental inspection of the proverbial gift-horse.

Mahon sets his most perfect brief vision of community on the island of Aran, beginning with a sketch of two folk-singers, a couple whose musical collaboration is also a relationship with each other and with their society.[34] The stanza is lightly, assonantally rhymed, and the relaxed rhythms of the line embody the folk-singer's own ease with himself and his surroundings: 'He is earthed to his girl, one hand fastened / in hers, and with his free hand listens, / An earphone, to his own rendition / singing the darkness into the light'. The 'Ecclesiastes' ejaculation, 'God!', recurs in a completely different tone, warm, admiring, a touch envious: 'God, that was the way to do it, / Hand-clasping, echo-prolonging poet!' Stronger rhyming in stanza 2 recreates 'that tradition' for a speaker who is 'Generations off the land': it closes on the beautiful correspondence of 'a loved hand in the other hand'. But the fantasy of incorporation is stifled. In stanza 3, a strange 'long glow' turns into a shocking, dissonant creature, 'A crack-voiced rock-marauder, scavenger, fierce / Friend to no slant fields or the sea either'. This semi-mythic creature, perhaps a heron, but surely embodying Baudelaire's poet-albatross, too, vanishes in an image of stunning negation as it 'Folds back over the forming waters' – isolation now revealed as the true mode of liberation.

Time for such a poet seems more comfortable than space. His fluent relocations and transmigrations allow him to inhabit history more fully than if his view had been simply topical or social. Mahon takes the long view as well as the oblique angle. Thus the starved, imprisoned, light-seeking mushrooms in the 'Disused Shed in Co. Wexford'[35] are identified with 'the lost people of Treblinka and Pompei', besides, implicitly, with the Irish subjects of political tryanny and intellectual darkness. The 'expropriated mycologist' might personify imperial decline; as well as the British Empire, those of the Third Reich and Rome. 'Let not our naïve labours have been in vain', suggests no particular community. 'Labours' might of course be associated with the *lumpen* proletariat and 'labour' in the Marxist sense, but the overriding impression is of a sheer, blind labouring to survive – the supra-historic, probably unending condition of the majority of organic life on earth, human and fungal. Yet Mahon's vision is not ahistorical. MacNeice, in Canto 9 of his great edge-of-war sequence, *Autumn Journal*, wrote a vivid, scrambling, novelistic portrait of what we might call 'every day life in classical Greece' which he concluded with the sardonic quatrain: 'And how one can imagine oneself among them / I do not know; / It was all so unimaginably different / And all so long ago'.[36] The point being, of course, that it was not: classical men and women were essentially the same as us. For Mahon's imagination, too, the past is recent. History – the flux of time and of the organism within time – receives the solitary figure into less troubled forms of community.

Poetic form also converses with a historical dimension. Its use connects the poet with writers of the past –as well as with like-minded peers. Yet it may also imply artistic isolation in a liberal contemporary ambiance. No writer coming of age in the sixties could fail to hear the arguments against form, certainly no writer as alert to the fractures of modernism as Mahon. Mahon seems attracted by iconoclastic approaches – from Beat poetry to the sociopoetics of Marxist-feminism, and, as a dramatist-translator, he has needed to keep a line open to the demotic. Radical politics positions itself as anti-formalist, with form being perceived as patriarchal, or at least antipathetic to spontaneous and fresh acts of communication, and reinforcing the notion of the poet as stuffed shirt in a tracksuit-and-trainers world. One of Mahon's internalised wars appears to be that of political liberalism and poetic rigour – a war whose confused origins make it no less virulent a force.

Mahon's *Yellow Book* poems discuss, sometimes ambivalently, the importance of poetic form. But the earlier work has, in one

20

way, resolved the argument. It contrives to be in dialogue not only with Larkin, but Beckett. Within its apparent symmetries, there is at times a destabilising process at work, almost as if scepticism about form were included in the existentialist's "consistent atheism". This occurs from an early point, so it is important to note that the "baggier" later work found in the sequences of 'Letters' does *not* signal a complete reversal of earlier techniques. Mahon is attracted, for example, to the asymmetry of the three-lined stanza. Not all these tercet-structured poems counter-balance themselves with rhyme. 'The Last of the Fire Kings' [37] is almost non-rhyming: the full chime of 'churns'/'turns' is an anomaly, indeed an asymmetry. The poem is breathlessly enjambed, though braced by the curt rhythms of the lines – mostly dimeter, occasionally monometer or trimeter. Twice near the end, tercet mutates into quatrain. There seems no formal or mimetic reason for this. Compared with the earlier, tercet-structured poem, 'Lives', which stuck to its established metre and tightened the weave with strong if sporadic patches of rhyme, it is a poem of controlled disintegration. The two occasions when the line is broken after the main verb ('to be' in both cases) testify to the ontological doubt the asymmetry embodies: 'I want to be / Like the man who descends / At two milk-churns' and 'Either way, I am / Through with history – '.

The engaging miniatures threaded together in the sequence *Light Music* vary from the strongly rhymed and metrically regular (e.g. 'Enter') to the metrically free and unrhymed ('Mozart'). Some of the little poems contrive both to rhyme and not rhyme: 'Donegal' for instance plays hide and seek with a microcosmic *terza rima*, finding and losing it in the briefest of moments: 'The vast clouds migrate / above turf-stacks / and a dangling gate.//A tiny bike squeaks / into the wind'.[38] On its more majestic scale, 'A Disused Shed in Co. Wexford' has similar asymmetries: the rhyming is held off altogether until six lines into stanza 1, and then seems to occur randomly, each stanza being differently though densely rhymed. By submitting to the random-within-the-form, a poem may evolve and vary like a living but skeletally bound organism.

The neat, brisk epistles of the 1960s and 70s might be packed with observation ('Beyond Howth Head', for instance) but it is

'The Yaddo Letter' which inaugurates the move from snapshots to cinema. Relinquishing neither his cultural pantheon nor his foreign vantage-points, Mahon begins to connect poetic conversation to family, and it's as if the chattier tone allowed had drawn him to the longer line and away from stanzaic convention. It's true that the more shaped poems of his 2005 collection, *Harbour Lights* continue the themes of family connection, but even here there are letter poems, sometimes spliced into long sections more paragraph than stanza (as well as poems with stanzas of eight or ten lines).

Spreading itself in long lines (iambic pentameter often mutating to alexandrine), the 'Yaddo' is the only letter in which the poet personally "signs off" ('My love, as ever, / – Daddy'), and one of the very few in which the recipient(s) are spoken to directly, as if expected to reply. The tender, jokey register suggests a man trying hard – even a shade too hard – to share his children's worlds and show them his.

> Do you still like your London schools? Do you
> still slam the goals in, Rory? Katie-coo
> how goes it with the piano and the flute?
> I've a composer in the next-door suite
> called Gloria (*in excelsis*), an English novelist,
> a sculptor from Vermont, a young ceramist
> from Kansas; for we come in suns and snows
> from *everywhere* to write, paint and compose.[39]

As the letter unfurls, variable rhymes as well as shifting rhythms assert Mahon's willingness to engage with the random. His couplet structure is not continuously enforced, and rhymes and half-rhymes may cluster in threes: 'I'd hoped to be more fun and try to write / you something entertaining as I often try to do; / but this time round I wanted to be *seerious* and true / to felt experience. My love 2U.'

In *The Hudson Letter*[40] the voice is more its poetic self, and the place more present. He describes Manhattan in broad brisk strokes, zapping from topic to topic less in the manner of a letter-writer than a TV travel-show presenter. The aim is neither empathy nor self-disclosure: rather it is entertainment and travelogue, spiced with the occasional wry confession. The pleasure of these poems is their almost greenhorn unselfconsciousness. Ex-pat poets with an eye on two audiences can get tempted into writing predictable all-pleasing reports, but Mahon is writing about *his* America, simply, and addressing his people – his friend, Patricia King, or his children. The loneliness of the "existential lyric" was never farther away.

The lines are so extended that Mahon needs a longer sentence than usual if he is to keep his syntactical rope in play. However, sheer colloquial energy often takes up the slack. As in *The Yaddo Letter* there are registers not heard before in his work. 'For I too have been homeless and in detox / with BAAAD niggaz 'n' crack hoes on the rocks'.[41] The vernacular is particularly zestful in the 'King Kong' description,[42] with quotes, jokes and gleeful asides delivered as if in popcorn-munching movie-realtime. Mahon has always responded to works of art as passionately as to artists, and now the range is extended to popular culture. But that pantheon of kindred artistic souls continues to hover, summoned by epigraph or quotation: P.J. O'Rourke, Louis MacNeice, Laforgue, Ovid, Turgenev, Auden, Elizabeth Bishop, Susan Sontag, Sappho, *inter alia*. And the letters are not purely vernacular: there are times when they discover an old oracular register, just as, decades ago, did the voice in 'Homecoming'.

The Yellow Book[43] leaves behind the New York glitter, and a chiefly Dublin location provides the setting for dystopian visions of the urban 90s. They vibrate unhappily with the 'venal roar' of a sophisticated technology that has become an exhausting plethora of images, logos, catchphrases, and all 'the pastiche paradise of the post-modern'. Such a hectic *dérive* risks being too stimulating: the centre only just holds. The rhythms are still vigorous and the rhymes, though irregularly spaced, emphatic. Welcome chill-out moments have characteristic rhetorical flair: the disarming advice of Chuang Tzu ('Do nothing; do nothing and everything will be done'), the portrait of Eugene Lambe ('one of those perfect writers who never write') and the journalistic tissue is richly embroidered with literary quotations and references.

Critics have been overly hard on *The Yellow Book*. Why shouldn't a brilliant formalist set out to explore rougher, more accumulative methods? Mahon's deliberate, poet-playwright's goal was a "conversational" style. As he says, 'The Greeks followed tragedies with Satyr plays'.[44] *The Yellow Book* is colourful, racy, mournful, nostalgic and often very funny in its jaundiced way, a bold capturing of 'the music of what happens' as performed by spoof post-punk rock-groups, 'Shit, Sperm, Garbage, Gristle, Scum'.[45] Other voices provide substantial interludes, via translation or monologue, and Larkin is a dolefully nudging presence: '...why / travel when imagination can get you there in a tick / and you're not plagued by the package crowd?...',[46] 'You might have thought them mature student, clerk / or priest once, long ago in the demure '60s / before the country first discovered sex'.[47] The mingling of historical and domestic affiliations may suggest Lowell in the rag-bag sonnet-sequences such as *The Dolphin* and *For Lizzie and Harriet*. However, MacNeice's big urban canvases are surely influential. Mahon's New York travelogue begins perhaps in 'Birmingham'.[48]

Occasionally the satire droops. A rather half-hearted listing of 'those desperate characters of the previous '90s' deflates the middle of 'Hangover Square' [49] after the fine, Wildean start. Mahon seems to have little enthusiasm left for the spirited delinquents of the 1890s, and none for himself. The modern decadent, who has survived so much, from sectarian violence to '*les amours jaunes*' – nicotine and booze, appears to have lost heart, though a scathingly witty couplet restores the poem's spirits for a time: 'Today is the first day of the rest of your life? / – tell that to your liver; tell that to your ex-wife.' Writing in the plural, half-speaking perhaps for his old Trinity friend, Michael Longley, as well as his 90s forebears, he seems uncertain whether to praise or deride the prosodic ideal of 'each verse coterminous with its occasion, / each line the pretext for a precious cadence'. He concludes that

> The most of what we did and wrote was artifice,
> rhyme-sculpture against the entangling vines of nature –
> a futile project since, in the known future,
> real books will be rarities in techno-culture,
> a forest of intertextuality like this...

The final image is of an ageing technophobe, as alienated from the micro-chip as he once was alienated from 'home', but less guiltily, less angrily. For all that he's 'sticking with' his typewriter, the speaker seems to have lost some fundamental belief to do with traditional form and the power of his singular rhetoric. Fatalistically, *The Yellow Book* permits 'the venal roar' to overwhelm the hard-won authority of solitude and art. Mahon resumes his stanzaic rhyme-sculpture in subsequent poems. 'St Patrick's Day' [50] with its nine large-scale Yeatsian stanzas, swiftly alighting historical grasp and collage-like layering of past and present, Dublin and New York, is love poem, birthday poem and meditation. But even here, in the penultimate stanza, the valedictory tone is unmistakeable. 'I now resign these structures and devices' is a pronouncement recalling Prospero's speech in Act Five of Shakespeare's *The Tempest*: 'But this rough magic / I here abjure'. However, the final stanza seems to "turn" away from valediction.

> The one reality is the perpetual flow,
> chaos of complex systems; each generation
> does what it must; middle age and misanthropy
> like famine and religion, make poor copy;
> and even the present vanishes like snow
> off a rope, frost off a ditch, ice in the sun –
> so back to the desk-top and the drawing-board,
> prismatic natural light, slow-moving cloud,
> the waves far thundering in a life of their own,
> a young woman hitching a lift on a country road'.

Fresh, regenerative horizons are embodied in the favourite Mahonian image of moving cloud no less than in the *aisling* of the hitch-hiking girl. And, as it turns out, this last stanza of the *Collected Poems* prefigures the recovery of formal and lexical energies (back to the drawing-board?) demonstrated in the succeeding volume *Harbour Lights* (2005). 'The Cloud Ceiling' [51] is exemplary: a stanzaic letter to the poet's newborn child which seems to mime the mysterious processes of birth and early consciousness in its cloud and star imagery. The turn at the end delivers its unsentimental insight with stunning casualness: 'So drench the nappies; fluff, bubble and burp: / I probably won't be here when you've grown up.' Mahon has always understood that 'the one reality is the perpetual flow' and the passage of urine and the passage of time make for a witty coupling.

Courage is not primarily a literary quality but it is part of the existentialist's moral enterprise to be poetically and humanly 'awake to the harsh stars for the cold truth'. Stoicism, balance – the classical virtues – underwrite not only his 'verse hard-wired' but the productive vacillations between the expansive and the minimalist, the formal and the de-formed, the anguished solitariness and the social responsibility, the single piercing image and the postmodern mish-mash. Mahon's work is essentially thanatopsist, if not elegiac, but its manner is buoyant. Cheerily, adroitly, it circles around that extreme human moment of isolation, death, while conjuring a sense of the placeless molecular interchange that will succeed individual extinction. So the title-poem[52] concludes with a welter of micro-organic activity: there is another baptismal 'drench' – this time 'a drenching of the wilful sperm' – and a Lucretian vision that trails off into mimetic ellipsis and question-mark: 'the millions swarming into pond and river/ to find the right place, find it and live for ever...?' The prospect of impersonality is not the prospect of dread, as it was for Larkin: organic breakdown is simply the ultimate expression of that sociable silence which the poet has always made his own. His poems too will be among companions.

NOTES

1. Derek Mahon, *Collected Poems* (Oldcastle: Gallery Press, 1999), p.70; hereinafter, *CP*.

2. 'The Existential Lyric', first published in *The New Statesman*, 1977, reprinted in Derek Mahon, *Journalism*, ed. Terence Brown (Oldcastle: Gallery Press, 1996), pp.55-57.

3. See, for example, Mahon's 'Heraclitus on Rivers', *CP*, p.114, and 'Lucretius on Clouds', Harbour Lights (Oldcastle: Gallery Press, 2005), p.21.

4. 'The Mute Phenomena', *CP*, p. 82.

5. *CP*, p.36.

6. 'Nostalgias', *CP*, p.75.

7. See, for example, poems 3, 4, 17, 19, 20 of 'Light Music', *CP*, pp.70-75.

8. Michael Longley, *Tuppenny Stung: Autobiographical Chapters* (Belfast, Lagan Press, 1994), p.33.

9. John Brown, 'Derek Mahon', *In the Chair: Interviews with Poets from the North of Ireland* (Cliffs of Moher, Co. Clare: Salmon Publishing, 2002), p.111.

10. *CP*, p.14.

11. *CP*, p.105.

12. Philip Larkin: unpublished autobiographical sketch, quoted in *Philip Larkin: A Writer's Life* (London: Faber, 1993), pp.13-15.

13. In the Chair, p.115.

14. *CP*, p.28.

26

15. Michael Longley, 'The Hebrides', *No Continuing City* (London: Macmillan, 1969).

16. Derek Mahon, 'The Banished Gods', *CP*, p.85.

17. *In the Chair*, p.91.

18. *CP*, p.17.

19. See 'North Wind: Portrush', *CP*, p.100.

20. *CP*, p.13.

21. *CP*, p.58.

22. *CP*, p.47.

23. Seamus Heaney, 'Digging', *Death of a Naturalist* (London: Faber, 1966).

24. Ciaran Carson, *Breaking News* (Oldcastle: Gallery Press, 2003).

25. *CP*, p. 33.

26. *CP*, p.35.

27. *CP*, p.51.

28. *CP*, p.52.

29. *CP*, p.29. Isis Oirr is the smallest of the Aran Islands.

30. W.H. Auden, *Another Time* (London: Faber, 1940).

31. Louis MacNeice, *Collected Poems*, ed. E.R. Dodds (London: Faber, 1991), p.84.

32. See *Wintering Out* (London: Faber, 1972) and also related poems about the Bog People in Heaney's *North* (London: Faber, 1975).

33. *CP*, p.44.

34. 'Aran', *CP*, p.37.

35. 'A Disused Shed in Co. Wexford', *CP*, p.89.

36. Louis MacNeice, *Collected Poems*, pp.117-19.

37. *CP*, p.64.

38. *CP*, pp.70-74.

39. *CP*, p.182.

40. *The Hudson Letter*, *CP*, pp 186-222.

41. XII 'Alien Nation'.

42. XIV 'Beauty and the Beast'.

43. *The Yellow Book*, *CP*, pp.223-64.

44. IX 'At the Gate Theatre'.

45. XI 'At the Chelsea Arts Club'.

46. II 'Axel's Castle'.

47. IV 'Shiver in Your Tenement'.

48. Louis MacNeice, *Collected Poems*, pp.17-18.

49. VIII takes its title from the novel by Patrick Hamilton, *Hangover Square*, 1941 (reissued London: Penguin Classics, 2001).

50. CP, p.285.

51. Derek Mahon, *Harbour Lights* (Oldcastle: Gallery Press, 2005), p.29.

52. *Harbour Lights*, p.61.

II *Philip Larkin's Lost Childhood*

In *The Untouched Key: Tracing Childhood Trauma in Creativity and Destructiveness,* the psychoanalyst Alice Miller finds connections between artistic work and repressed early experiences.[1] For example, in December 1884, in Malaga, Picasso and his family had to flee an earthquake. A few days later, the three-year-old boy was present when his mother gave birth to his sister. Miller links both earth-quake and birth-quake to the bodily fragmentation and jolts of focus in the painting, *Guernica*. Picasso's later Cubist works, for Miller, continue to reflect the scenes of physical disruption the child uncomprehendingly observed. 'Where is the foot? Where is the hand? Why are the eyes placed so they aren't looking at us, so that they aren't looking at anyone?' While the popular view of Picasso at 90, still painting his distorted females nudes, was that he was obsessed with sex, Miller believes he was compulsively recreating those early images. She gives a similarly childhood-based account of the mournful mothers and frail gaunt children repeatedly found in the work of Kathe Kollwitz, whose mother lost three children in infancy. Childhood trauma, a life-shaping drama for everyone, may in fact be a work-shaping drama for creative artists, particularly if the memory of the original experiences and emotions is suppressed.

For many writers, childhood is an examined influence. The experience may be conscripted to stories of the self and its development with a view to demonstrating transcendence, as in the case of the motherless Wordsworth, re-mothered by his beloved landscape, or it may reveal the inescapability of a tragic narrative pattern, as in the case of Sylvia Plath.

Philip Larkin subverts both traditions. In his mature poetry he implies that he is a writer *sans* childhood. Striking opacities occur in his style when he picks up the theme. Typically, it is subjected to a sonorous statement, labelled with negative or abstract nouns, and quickly discarded: 'Life is first boredom', 'forgotten boredom', 'wrong beginnings', 'nothing', 'unspent'. Larkin's poetic story of himself includes the nullity of his childhood and the nullity of his childlessness – the latter, a subject of pained, humorous interrogation, the former, a matter of vague hints. His one contribution to the childhood-memory poem is a harsh satire on the genre, 'I Remember, I Remember', with its chant of epiphanies that did not happen.[2]

This poem does not merely mock a sentimental genre. With a male, philistine sneer, it mocks the vulnerability of writers and writing: it mocks *him*. Larkin, writing autobiographically at his own admission, clearly could have claimed *some* formative imaginative experiences. That he did not 'invent / blinding theologies of flowers and fruits', for example, is belied by his romantic teenaged nature-poems, in which sun, trees, clouds, sky seem almost mystic presences. But the whole baby is thrown out with the soapy water, leaving a man-sized hole. '"Was that," my friend smiled, "Where you 'have your roots'?"/ No, only where my childhood was unspent, / I wanted to retort...' There's a staggering mixture of desolation and humorous suppression in that term 'unspent', an unusual negative, one of Larkin's brilliant coinages. It tells us that the childhood was not only lacking in event. It was cancelled, or stolen. It was not – though, in the poem's imaginary dialogue, the protagonist does not even get as far as this comment ('I *wanted* to retort').

Larkin's most direct account of his childhood is a memoir that seems to have evolved out of a survey of his still uncrystallised writing ambitions, jotted down in 1945 when he was 23. Never published in its entirety, the piece is quoted at some length by Andrew Motion in his biography.[3] It begins: 'When I try to tune into my childhood, the emotions I pick up are, overwhelmingly, *fear* and *boredom*.' (*My italics*.)

Childhood will be described as a 'forgotten boredom' in the 1950 poem, 'Coming',[4] and, 13 years later, in 'Dockery and Son',[5] the contention will be that 'Life is first boredom, then fear', but it is only in this memoir that Larkin appears to connect both terms, boredom and fear, with childhood. In the thumbnail biography sketched by the poem, boredom clearly belongs to childhood, while fear relates to adolescent (and adult) angst. In the memoir, the fact that 'fear' is named first in the sentence, suggests that it dominates the writer's memory. Not that Larkin directly attributes the fear (or the boredom) to himself. It is something he *picks up*, like a radio antenna, from the atmosphere. It might as well be his elder sister's or his mother's, or his father's, as his own. When he links it to his own experience, it is only indirectly.

With a flicker of aphoristic humour, he generalises the Larkin household as 'dull, pot-bound and slightly mad'. But no affectionate Alan Bennett-like portrait of family eccentrics ensues. What he sets down is primarily an account of a deeply miserable marriage.

'As I picture him,' Larkin says of his father, cooling to his theme, '(he) was intensely shy, inhibited not robust, devoid of careless sensual instincts (though not of humour)'. While Sidney 'worked all day and shut himself away reading in the evening', his mother, Eva, 'constantly toiled at "running the house", a task that was always beyond her...' At one point, he recollects, she 'sprang up from the table announcing her intention to commit suicide'.

Pathetically, or disingenuously, Larkin blames himself for his poor relationship with his father: 'Second child, myself, lived in a private world, disregarding what awkward overtures he could make, and was handicapped by an embarrassing stammer...' He is in fact almost stammering on the page but then the blockage clears and the earlier attempt at even-handedness gives way to tentative accusation. 'His personality had imposed that taut ungenerous defeated pattern of life on the family, and it was only to be expected that it would make them miserable and that their misery would react on him'.

Larkin finishes by saying that his childhood has left him with 'two convictions: that human beings should not live together and that children should be taken from their parents at an early age'. Out of context, this sounds like comic exaggeration, but the bitterness of the earlier paragraphs also lends it a tone of brutal solution. It prefigures the conclusion of 'This Be The Verse':[6] 'Get out as early as you can / And don't have any kids yourself.' The memoir, too, has that odd, voice-throwing characteristic, as if a polite ventriloquist suffered an anarchic dummy squawking interruptions.

'This Be The Verse' was written 25 years later. For all the poem's assurance, it is not only the diction that is violently unsettled. The imagery too shifts alarmingly, from the cartoon Victorians of the 2nd stanza, either 'soppy-stern' or 'at one another's throats', to the odd geological simile introduced by the hieratic (and Victorian-sounding) pronunciation of the last stanza: 'Man hands on misery to man. / It deepens like a coastal shelf.' The poem is closer to absurdism than cheery comedy (if miseries and fuck-ups were really building cumulatively from generation to generation human life would by now be non-existent). At the same time it contains a compelling portrait of the poisoned economy of a family in which the parents, themselves psychologically wounded, wound the child, who subsequently refuses to continue the process. The first stanza, with its assertive statement and slightly timid qualification ('They may not mean to but they do'), suggests a male-female dialogue, though there is no serious disagreement between the voices. The coinage 'soppy-stern' itself is a merging of stereotypical female-male characteristics.

Larkin's deeper sympathies as an artist are always with the anima (the Jungian term for the feminine aspect of character) There is a strong indication that he believed that in order to be a writer he needed to be a kind of woman. In a short play written in 1950, 'Round the Point: Debat Inedit', one of two pieces based on the Socratic Dialogue, the novelist-character, Geraint, asserts: 'The writer is feminine. His attitude to life is passive. He is recording wax or litmus paper, and should not try to select what he is going to experience, always provided that it leaves him able to write.' [7] Note the proviso, a hint, perhaps, that if something like marriage offered itself, passive acceptance would not be appropriate! In fact the anima, docile and despairing, could not provide the male writer's full complement of poetic tone. When, in the memoir, he characterises his mother as 'an obsessive snivelling pest' who delivers 'monstrous whining monologues', these phrases might give us a moral shudder but add welcome shots of vitality to the drab analysis. Similarly in the poetry, which at first is oracular and vague. Once Larkin is able to integrate the hard, mean jokiness of the animus (Sidney's 'humourless yap of laughter') with the lyricism, or at least to allow them to co-exist within a single poem, his writing receives the energy-boost that engenders style. It's as if the poet rescues and remakes his parents' marriage into an artistic whole – a surrogate union that actually getting married might have prevented.

In 'Dockery and Son', the poetic charge occurs when mimicry ceases we feel the narrator's whiplash of self-pity: 'For Dockery, a son, for me nothing, / Nothing with all a son's harsh patronage.' The compression of rhetorical devices here, zeugma and anadiplosis, reinforces the sense of anguish. The hidden personification of childlessness is stunningly effective: this 'nothing' is a kind of child itself, dominating and demanding. It is also one of the cruellest kinds of child – the son that mocks the father, the son that Larkin could sometimes be. As in 'This Be The Verse', the extraordinary parent, the poet, seems to identify with and feel at least a cool compassion for the ordinary parent who bore him.

Larkin's most forceful poems are argumentative, or at least make space for other speakers, inner and external. An unattributed voice will briefly cut into a poem's monologue, or be brought up from its sound-track: '*Now, dear child, what's wrong?*' in 'Faith Healing',[8] the words of a hymn in 'The Explosion'.[9] The speaker may draw non-poetic voices from himself. 'Surely he's taken her home by now' is an interjection in 'Love Again' though it's the speaker's own.[10] Or he may pose a question and answer it, as in the first stanza of 'Days': 'What are days for? / Days are where we live.'[11] Poetically, such devices are beautifully strategic. They create variety-within-unity and natural colloquial or rhetorical effects: they add an attractive, authentic worldliness to the lyricism. But, as we've seen in 'This be the Verse' it can also be disturbing when the poems mix voices or registers without resolving them. So the reader is jolted, in the five quatrains of 'High Windows', from the demotic 'When I see a couple of kids / And guess he's fucking her...' to the hieratic 'deep blue air, that shows / Nothing, and is nowhere, and is endless'.[12] As before, the conflict is not just one of register; here, it is a shift between realism and symbolism. Larkin also writes a quieter kind of poem, often liked least by his critics because such poems are supposedly the most "English", which celebrates unity and peace. Might the two placid race-horses, retired in the 'unmolesting meadows' of 'At Grass'[13] symbolise the resolved marital quarrel? The lovely spring-welcoming, bird-imitating poem 'Coming' clearly alludes to marital reconciliation, as a vivid wish or even a memory breaks through the willed fog, the 'forgotten boredom', and the speaker compares himself to 'a child / Who comes on a scene / Of adult reconciling, / And can understand nothing / But the unusual laughter, / And starts to be happy'.[14]

Larkin's quest to find his personal tone was notoriously protracted. He sought literary mentors as various as Eliot, Lawrence, Vernon Watkins, Yeats, Hardy, Auden, Kingsley Amis, Evelyn Waugh. I include novelists because there was also the bigger question – that of genre. Was he a novelist or a poet? (He originally considered himself to be primarily a novelist.) Another early debate was the sexual one. Did he embody more of the anima or the animus? Was he heterosexual or homosexual? These arguments, resolved at the level of daily life, remain in secret interplay throughout his work.

Larkin's mature poetry is of course immensely controlled. It may grumble unexpected obscenities, it may show us disturbing images, but its tone remains urbane, its forms unshattered. He is no Cubist. It is easy to read him as a realist. But Larkin's realism hides a mythical distortion, and underlying his most powerful poems is a pervasive sense of mortal entrapment. The question 'Where shall we live but days?' is horrifying if you peep under its rhetorical veil. For the existentialist, there should exist nothing outside time. Larkin's atheism, unlike Derek Mahon's, seems burdened by a vestigial belief in personal continuity. Death prompts further claustrophobia, because it is imagined in terms of time. High windows, light, arrow-showers, etc. signify an escape-route but these erotic and (I believe) homosexual symbols are poetic visions of the unattainable. Time, for Larkin, is steady movement towards death or fearful stasis. These sensations suggest the gloomy household of the 1945 memoir, where fear and boredom fuse in the child's unmediated, time-uncomprehending perspective. Adolescence will offer vistas of opportunity and departure, but the primary, psychologically engrained experience – and the primary insight of the poetry – is based on the child's irrational fear that there is no escape.

The poems of Larkin's late adolescence state many of the themes of the mature poetry. Though skilfully imitative in style, they contain original and acute self-analyses, and demonstrate how some of the problems, literary and psychological, operate within various social contexts.

A sonnet written early in 1940, 'Nothing significant was really said',[15] reveals the 18-year-old poet's fascination with the gifted failure. The octet depicts a brilliant young 'freshman' who impresses his friends with his eloquence, and seems assured of future success. The sestet however takes the point of view of a knowing comrade, who has caught the brilliant talker off guard, in lamentations: 'O what unlucky streak / Twisting inside me made me break the line? / What was the rock my gliding childhood struck, / And what bright unreal path has led me here?' Both nature and nurture are blamed: an 'unlucky streak' which is inborn and creates a contortion inside the speaker's psyche that forces him to 'break the line' and an exterior factor, a rock which has deflected a calmly 'gliding childhood'. Shipwreck is implied, a sea metaphor that possibly prefigures the 'coastal shelf' of 'This Be The Verse'

Larkin was not yet an Oxford undergraduate, and his third-person narrative does not necessarily conceal a projection into his own future. He is not, at this stage in his development, a lone writer, or one who habitually writes only about himself. The poems he produced in late adolescence sometimes name contemporaries – a sporadic series of 'Stanley' poems for example, addressed to a schoolmate, Ernest Stanley Saunders. Some have the plural pronoun. The two poems that immediately predate the sonnet are clearly love poems. The emphasis on spoiled opportunity however establishes a characteristic angle for the poet's self-searching. If the 'gliding childhood' was in fact Larkin's, was the rock his parents' monstrous marriage – or some specific childhood event? We might look into the public arena as well for a further alternative.

Slightly later than 'Nothing significant was really said', 'Poem: Study in Four Parts'[16] ambitiously correlates war and spoiled childhood. Larkin has been under-read as a war poet, unsurprisingly, since his war poems are part of his juvenilia, but the public trauma of 1939-45 cannot be discounted as one of the roots of his forlorn determinism (with the added complication, of course, of Sydney's Nazi sympathies). The poem begins with an image of mass slaughter ('When so many dropped on the harsh / Morning between our century's two nights / Have died like a rag on a nail...'), then pits the individual (himself or his beloved) against history's depradations: 'Which of the death-saddened ears will note / A single body's achievement of nineteen years?' This poignantly conveys the alienation young people inevitably experience as they come of age and inherit a culture not of their own making. Such an experience must be particularly acute during war-time. Larkin would no doubt have thought even then of the possibility of his own conscription (in the event, three years later, he failed the army medical on account of his short-sightedness). But it does not seem to be war alone that spoils childhood in this poem: 'One difficult day a sleep-walking child / Woke in the house of mirrors, // Saw its name signed / As receiving a load of years; saw the new oil / In the new engines getting greater power; / Saw with a start / Its interesting face, and the faces of all the others.' The Lacanian image of mirroring becomes sexually charged, only to result in disappointment: the shattering of the mirrors and the loss of a mysterious path, 'all eaten with flowers'. This section concludes with further war imagery, as 'columns of marching men' disappear into the hill, 'thicker and brighter than wheat' – an image which looks ahead, in its subdued and oblique eroticism, to that of 'postal districts / Packed like squares of wheat' in 'The Whitsun Weddings'.[17] The impediment to the flourishing of youthful hope may not be war alone, but the sense that the homoerotic path can no longer be followed.

Part III also has a moment of foreshadowing: when the poet wishes the loved one a bird that will become 'a scarlet target, afloat / For the strength of your striking arrow' the 'arrow-shower' of the later poem comes to mind. But this section is interesting for other reasons: it is where the key phrase 'forgotten childhood' makes its debut.

> For the time of heroics is past,
> Farther than our forgotten childhoods,
> Those acid summers of the twenties
> When Lawrence still saw hope for some of us,
> But died before the thirties stamped it out...

The context seems benign: the plural 'our forgotten childhoods' indicates a shared, almost conspiratorial forgetfulness. Teenaged boys, possibly lovers, have no need of childhood memories. But the linking of 'acid summers' with the reference to Lawrence could suggest that the speaker's imagination is being pulled back into the personal realm. That interesting adjective 'acid' evokes clever, stinging wit (as in 'acid remark'), a quality we might associate with the bright, anxious decade of the 1920s, but also stomach-burning anger, which might belong nearer home.

Larkin came to mock the Lawrence who mattered so much to him in youth. 'I Remember, I Remember' in fact 'started off as a satire on novels like *Sons and Lovers* – the kind of wonderful childhoods that people do seem to have'.[18] But Lawrence was a key figure for Larkin's early development. 'To me Lawrence is what Shakespeare was to Keats and all the other buggers' he enthused to Jim Sutton.[19] And he announced, *a propos* of his hero, that 'there has been a change in the English psyche. The wind is blowing "in a new direction of time" and I feel that you & I who will be if anyone the new artists, are onto it.' The tone of this letter is hardly pessimistic. So it is interesting that two years earlier, in 'Poem: Study in Four Parts', Larkin had already decided the Lawrentian hope had been 'stamped out'.

The poem is imbued with that sense of unfulfilled promises, of positive things happening too late or being spoiled– the ache of disappointment that we will come to think typical of Larkin. The letter boasts of future artistic achievement, which Larkin of course will attain, but implies a revolutionary iconoclasm which he won't. Whatever the nature of the hope Lawrence saw for the young (greater naturalness of upbringing, guiltless sexual expression, perhaps), the poem already knows that this particular road cannot be taken.

Lawrence is the likely source of Larkin's newly-discovered relish for colloquialism (it occurs much earlier in the letters than the poems). By the time he wrote to Sutton, he had read not only the novels ('the greatest') and the newly collected *Letters*, but the *Fantasia of the Unconscious*, Lawrence's extraordinary polemic on child-rearing and family psychology, in which, in a chapter called 'The Vicious Circle', the family is described as 'an intimate mesh of love, love-bullying and spiritual incest'.[20] Knowing as much as we do about Larkin's view of his own home-life, we can safely assume the *Fantasia* struck some familiar chords. A complicating factor for Larkin must have been that Lawrence was one of his father's favourite writers, too.

Lawrence was never a poetic model for Larkin. What he gave him, apart, perhaps, from the courage of his four-letter words, was a concept of the unconscious and a sense of its relationship with his other major enthusiasm, jazz. It was Auden who demonstrated how formal poetry, the sonnet in particular, could allegorise the psychological quest. Larkin's early work aspires to the scope of Eliot but finds a lyric safe haven in Auden. There was a further coincidental discovery – the work of Auden's friend, and one-time lover, the anthropologist and psychologist John Layard. A series of lectures was given at Oxford by Layard in 1942, followed a year later by a talk on Jung's 'The Night Journey over the Sea', bringing Larkin into fruitful contact with Jungian dream-analysis. Layard had been a disciple of Homer Lane and, according to the Auden scholar Edward Mendelson, 'preserved transcripts of his teachings as sacred texts'.[21]

The central tenet, opposite to Freud's, was that human impulses were essentially good, and that failure to act on them produced neurosis and illness ('Syphilis results from sexual guilt, cancer from foiled creativity.') Layard did not consider sublimation of sexual desire a 'civilising virtue' but preached liberation through enactment. For him, as for Lawrence, desires were God, and conscious control of them, evil. In the autumn of 1942 Larkin and some fellow Jungians embarked on a project to record and analyse their dreams. 'I have never read a book of psychology in my life...' Larkin later told Sutton 'But I can read the history of my soul in my dreams and whoever says I can't is a fucking liar... Insofar as psychology is a religion I accept and believe it. Insofar as it is a science I reject it utterly... We – you and I and anyone else who cares to come along – must stick to mysticism, religion, and the poetic unconscious.' He adds that he has written down and analysed 95 of his dreams and is 'still going strong'.[22]

The dream studies are part of his quest for sexual identity, and one in particular stands out. Dream 28, recorded on November 14th, 1942, describes a high, brightly lit room in a house which belongs to Christopher Isherwood. 'The panelling was white; the windows were high up in the walls, through which I could

37

see blue sky and the sun shone: the ceiling was immensely high, and the bookshelves went out of sight, away up the walls. It was a beautiful room.' Larkin gazes up and up, grows dizzy, and falls. Later he tries to get back to the room because there had been a piano there he wanted to play. 'I got back to it but it was all in darkness and I couldn't find the switch. In the next room two women were talking and laughing. I got frightened and ran away, only running my hand down the keyboard once'.[23] The imagery of the dream-room reappears on numerous entranced poetic occasions of sky, windows, light, etc. and, since the room belonged to Isherwood, it is reasonable to connect it with homosexuality, idealised and denied. In 'Dry-Point',[24] it may perhaps be subsumed into 'that bare and sunscrubbed room, / Intensely far, that padlocked cube of light', described by James Booth as 'one of the most evocative "unreal" rooms in Larkin's poetry' and one from which 'sexuality with all its complications is excluded'.[25] Such images generally oppose or transform a sexual context, suggesting perhaps the Platonic ideal of the soul's journey beyond (homo)erotic love into the realm of pure philosophy. The reverse process occurs when the arrow-shower at the end of 'The Whitsun Weddings' merely turns into earth-bound rain.

The 1942 poem, 'Conscript',[26] dedicated to Jim Sutton, is an Auden-Lawrence fable in which the hero, the inheritor of a relaxed and orderly landscape symbolising 'the ego's county', is one day accosted by 'a bunch of horsemen' who speak an unfamiliar dialect, and tell him that he is responsible for causing a war and must fight on their side. He agrees, but explains that his assent

> Was founded on desire for self-effacement
> In order not to lose his birthright; brave,
> For nothing would be easier than replacement,
>
> Which would not give him time to follow further
> The details of his own defeat and murder.

The view that the Ego should willingly join forces with the guerrilla-like horsemen of the Id, rather than maintain the truth-denying split between rational and creative forces, testifies to the Lawrence/Layard interpretation of psychic health. However, the result foreseen is hardly positive. Avoiding 'replacement', which implies progeny, the marriage and fatherhood that, quite literally, 'would not give him time' for the writing, the speaker opts for expression of his 'birthright', which is psychologically essential. However, his subject will be his own destruction.

This brings us back to the household of the 1945 memoir, in which childhood was metaphorically defeated and murdered, and leads me to the question of whether there was a physical component to the psychological maltreatment. The issue is raised more directly in one of Larkin's last poems, 'Love Again', in which the speaker blames his present sexual wretchedness on 'Something to do with violence / A long way back, and wrong rewards / And arrogant eternity'. Opinionated adjectives here add resonance to the bald abstract nouns, 'rewards' and 'eternity', while 'violence' seems to emerge from the same ugly stable as 'defeat and murder'.[27]

The critic and poet Grevel Lindop makes a thoroughly convincing case for tracing the phrase 'something to do with violence' to Auden's sonnet, 'A.E. Housman':[28]

> Deliberately he chose the dry-as-dust,
> Kept tears like dirty postcards in a drawer;
> Food was his public love, his private lust
> Something to do with violence and the poor.[29]

'Something to do with', a common enough colloquialism, stands out in both poetic contexts as euphemism or litotes. It conceals what is better not said, perhaps better not thought about. Auden's carefully chosen zeugma, 'violence and the poor', is of course a coded reference to his subject's homosexuality, the practice of which almost certainly included sado-masochism, and certainly involved contacts with working-class men. Like Larkin, Housman cherished a stash of porn: we are told it included such classics of sexual perversion as 'The Whippingham Paper'.[30] Auden, as a homosexual insider, clearly understands the exact nature of Housman's 'private lust' and his imprecision here strikes a note of *pas devant les enfants*. Disingenuously, or from simple tact, he lets his readers, if they are sufficiently worldly, fill in the details.

The leading question is what Larkin means by 'violence'. Lindop observes that 'it seems reasonable to take it that Larkin in these awkwardly phrased lines is attributing the failure of love to the pressure exerted by the rewards and demands of art, in which case the 'violence / a long way back' may have been the emotional violence involved in a decisive rejection of love in favour of art'. As Housman's unhappiness was always linked to the loss of his first love, Moses Jackson, so, Lindop reasons, Larkin's is linked to the cruelly conducted rejection of his first love, Ruth Bowman.

Possibly. But biographical evidence and the early poems demonstrate that Larkin's first love or loves were homosexual (Ernest Saunders at school, Philip Brown at Oxford, possible others). The Housman-Jackson connection more logically leads to the interpretation of 'violence' as self-violence, i.e. the deliberate stifling of the homosexual impulse, motivated by fear of his parents' disapproval and rejection, perhaps. It could of course imply that the erotic expression was itself violent or imaginatively associated with violence.

A simpler possibility is that, if the 'something to do with violence' happened 'a long way back', it connects to punitive treatment in Larkin's childhood. In 'Love Again' the word 'violence' ends the line and seems more shocking and mimetic than in the Auden poem, where it is smoothly blended into the rhythmic texture. The first syllable of the word has an almost physical jolt. The last two weak syllables and the natural end-of-line pause give extra time in which to let the slow, horrible impact sink in.

Larkin himself acknowledged the performative aspect of poetry and perhaps 'Love Again' should not be read as 'Larkin's Life Again' – except that there are those blanks which a more feigning, more self-dramatising poem would surely fill. Guilt, violence, blame, shame – all hover around the poem's last stanza unlocated. It is impossible not to connect them biographically – not to think they are demanding such connection.

Do we really 'know enough about his childhood to be sure his parents never beat or otherwise abused him', as Lindop claims? Larkin's biographers universally agree that he was not treated violently at home, but they do not address the question of whether he received corporal punishment, either at home or in school. The word 'reward' inevitably conjures its opposite: punishment.

Of course, the 'wrong rewards' may be the rewards of art

that militated against the rewards of love. 'Arrogant' might be a misplaced epithet, signifying the risk of hubris in having posterity as a goal for one's work. However, 'wrong rewards' also suggests being wrongly rewarded, by punishments, or by the encouragement of behaviour that is more for the parents' benefit than the child's. Punishment derives from the morality which is traditionally underwritten by concepts of 'arrogant eternity'. This last phrase, vaguest of all, might simply express Larkin's death terror in a new manner, personifying the overweening timelessless of non-being that so often accompanies his 'night-thoughts'. In the most depressing reading, it spells the final apotheosis and unavailability of the 'beautiful room'.

It is interesting in the context to look at the passages describing corporal punishment in the early Lesbian novella, *Trouble at Willow Gables*.[31] Here, the melodramatic tone in the chapter describing a miscreant's beating suggests an undercurrent of authorial sexual excitement. Perhaps it is significant that, in the sequel novella, where the Willow Gables schoolgirls are now living in a women's college in Oxford, the studious, rather remote character named Philippa develops an obsession with collecting belts. In a letter to Kingsley Amis, written in the summer of 1945, Larkin alludes to a game in which he and Bruce Montgomery, fantasising the subjects of their future novels, listed on the back of an envelope as many sexual perversions as they could think of. Larkin, as he reports, 'scored heavily with the inclusion of mastigopohily'.[32] 'Mastigophily' means the love of whips and whipping.

Sidney Larkin was the youngest of seven sons in an ambitious working-class family. It is extremely unlikely that he never experienced corporal punishment. Largely self-educated, he grew into a driven, obsessive man. Though he was intelligent and literary (and, in his own view, extremely shy) his background and character do not suggest he would have been a soft liberal in his views on child-rearing. Corporal punishment was, any how, part of the accepted behaviour of the time. It was not considered a form of abuse, as it is today: many parents saw it as a painful duty. Lawrence himself advocated it in his *Fantasia*. What Alice Miller dubs 'poisonous pedagogy' carries on from generation to generation, as parents, concealing their own damage under good disciplinarian intentions, mete out the same punishments they once received. The fact that Larkin stuttered as a child might indicate that he had learned fear in a context more immediately personal than the general war-zone atmosphere of his parents' marriage.

The belt is of course the traditional father's implement of chastisement. When children are beaten, the greater damage is usually psychological, involving crossed wires of pain and sexual stimulus. Larkin the poet does not take pleasure in others' suffering, but there is a certain amount of relish for his own: 'Depression is to me what daffodils were to Wordsworth' he notoriously once said. Depression, psychiatrists tell us, is internalised rage. Rage is unlikely to have been permitted in Larkin's household.

He was a wanted and somewhat favoured child but the repressive, isolating nature of his upbringing was clearly unfavourable to his independent development. Though not, strictly, an only one (his sister was eleven years his senior) he lacked friends – as, apparently, did his mother and father. He seems even in adulthood to have regarded his parents with all the intensity and idealisation felt by an only child. In both cases their deaths resulted in poetic silence, temporary when his father died, but final after the death of his mother. Andrew Motion goes so far as to claim Eva as Larkin's most significant Muse.[33]

The 1945 memoir reminds us that the major emotional connection was always the maternal one. It is worth quoting in full the passage that describes Eva's unconcealed misery. 'My mother, as time went on, began increasingly to complain of her dreary life...the monotonous whining monologue she treated my father to before breakfast, and all of us at mealtimes, resentful, self-pitying, full of funk and suspicion, must have remained in my mind as something I mustn't *under any circumstances* risk encountering again'.[34] The passage he underlined tells us not only why he determined to remain single, but that one of the things he feared so much as a child was upsetting his mother. Eva's depression was severe enough, we should remember, to have prompted a suicide threat. The effect of such parent-protective roles is damaging, however far removed from wilful cruelty. Alice Miller observes that such children, forbidden to express their anger, 'are compelled to suppress their feelings, repress all memory of the trauma, and idealise those guilty of abuse.

Later they will have *no memory of what was done to them*.[35]

Before finishing with the issue of abuse, I'd like to turn to a pre-1939 poem, 'Having grown up in shade of Church and State'.[36] Its protagonist is a prim, correct, slightly pampered, cricket-playing schoolboy, who 'smiles demurely at his uncle's jokes / And reads the *Modern Boy* in bed at night'. In the sestet, the boy is shown batting on the cricket pitch, and an unattributed voice, possibly the uncle's, exclaims, 'Y'know, he's good! Why, that's / A graceful player!' to which the speaker laconically responds: 'True? Perhaps. Benign, / We diagnose a case of good old sex'.

The sonnet is masterly and elegant. Whether or not we identify the child with Larkin, we recognise the stifling mix of privilege and correctness. It's not quite clear, in the sestet, if the sexuality, the 'case of good old sex', is the boy's (he could be flirting in his careful, graceful game) but that it is the spectator's response seems more likely. The young player may be skilful, but the voice is not commenting on his sportsmanship, in the opinion of the knowing narrator. 'A case of good old sex' is a quotation from Evelyn Waugh's *Decline and Fall*, in which one of the characters is explaining the nature of an aristocratic woman's relationship with her black footman.[37]

Does the sonnet's curious conclusion encode a personal acquaintance with adult sexuality in some shape or form? The use of the word, 'benign' is faintly worrying. In the poem, 'Deceptions',[38] the speaker identifies most intensely with the raped child. He enters her mind, conveys her violation from the inside. Then, words fail him, as they do in 'Love Again': 'What can be said, / Except that suffering is exact, but where / Desire takes charge, readings will grow erratic?' (In 'Love Again' he asks 'why put it into words?'). Though the narrator knows it is immaterial to the suffering child, the crux of the poem, which some readers dislike, lies in his perception that she was in fact 'less deceived' than her violator, 'stumbling up the breathless stair / To burst into fulfilment's desolate attic'.

An abused child might indeed be expected to show sympathy with the abuser: in some cases, at least, the sympathy would be part of the act demanded. It is interesting that 'Deceptions' is so deeply understanding of both points of view (and to its credit). The earlier poem might be read in a similar way. The 'benign' knowingness of its conclusion could spring from a young man's smilingly superior pose as he flaunts his adult reading, drawing on the Freudian idea of sublimation and the amused worldliness of Evelyn Waugh as proof of his sophistication – or it could express an oddly cheerful understanding of an older man's paedophilia.

Sadly, Larkin's creative fertility had a short life-span, almost as if subject to the same limitations as the female ovarian cycle. Perhaps Eva, muse and anima, really imprinted him with some kind of psychosomatic pattern. His fear of death deepened and confrontation in his work did not neutralise its power. As I suggested earlier, it seems that his greatest dread was the annihilation of sensation, not so much death as an unending coma-stricken consciousness of not-being. Another fear was embodied by his xenophobia. It is scarcely found in the poems but since its expression in the letters has had such an impact, it is worth noting the relationship of the two phobias. Recent research suggests that increased awareness of death ('mortality salience') results in a subject's greater dislike of people perceived as outsiders, and closer identification with his or her own cultural group.[39] If Larkin's racism really went beyond the cultural norm for his class and time (I am not convinced that it did) perhaps it was aggravated by the sense of encroaching death. It was also part of a general decline.

Mostly what he wrote in his last decade shows a narrowing and closing of mental arteries. He was unable to respond to new poetry, new jazz, new ideas. The sardonic, cruel, joking voice got louder. And the culture in which Larkin worked, the university culture, was just beginning to undergo its own processes of intellectual compromise under the leadership of the Prime Minister he claimed to 'adore' (Margaret Thatcher).

Larkin in a sense became his parents' marriage – of anger and funk. But, for a few slim decades, and a few slim volumes, he made wonderful art out of the broken self. He was, and still is, a presence, first loved for the wrong simplistic reasons and later despised for another set of wrong simplistic reasons. For some people he represents England– all its courage and civility or all its insular crassness and repression. The poetry, admittedly, has its nostalgic moments, but pastoral (for instance) does not demand to be read as imperial. The conservatism that is a form of conservationism should be distinguished from imperialism. Admittedly he helped promote the parodic Larkin. Perhaps it was another means of concealing himself from himself.

Larkin owns the English language in a peculiarly unjudgemental way. He allows its idiolects to jar at times, but the other side of the coin is polyphony, and in many poems he makes a seamless cloth of the motley that is Anglo-Saxon physicality, Latinate abstraction, and the man-in-the-street's low-key demotic.

English invites both compression and ramification, its syntax dogged by a picky clockwork of pronouns, prepositions, articles and cases of the verb 'to be', all of which resist the aphoristic fleetness of its naturalised stanza forms and rhetorical tropes. Larkin simply goes with the flow. He finds his subject in the everyday world, stuffs it with nouns, sends it with a magical gesture of rhetoric or metaphor flying away then brings it down to earth, 'somewhere becoming rain'. Lyrical desire and blunt scepticism lean quietly into each other. The intellect is open-ended notwithstanding his love of cadence and closure, self-critical where it evidently hurts. Beyond nostalgia, he is ruthless, indeed existentialist, in his secular honesty.

The finer details of Larkin's upbringing are now irretrievable. I hope I have demonstrated that there are solid grounds for questioning the assumption that he experienced no abuse beyond a lonely childhood in a squabbling, sterile marriage, and that, even if that had been the case, the effects were deeply injurious and should be taken into account when reading his character and his poetry. The heavy focus of the early work on psychic quest, the poetically important distortions of the realistic picture he set out to paint, are indicative. They are sign-posts to his past which seem to have been deliberately planted – and then deliberately left blank. Read in the light of extreme darkness, his poetry is not undermined but revealed in more fascinating detail, and our sense of the integrity and courage of his life's work enhanced. The young Philip Larkin, internalising the quarrel of his parents, and his own more loving and anxious quarrel *with* his parents, struck a psychic rock, but it was this that set him on his 'bright, unreal path' of evolution into that complex being, 'Philip Larkin, writer'.[40]

NOTES

1. Alice Miller, *The Untouched Key: Tracing Childhood Trauma in Creativity and Destructiveness*, tr. Hildegarde & Hunter Hannum (London: Virago Press, 1990), pp 3-35.

2. Philip Larkin, *Collected Poems*, ed. Anthony Thwaite (London: Faber, 1988), p.81; hereinafter, *CP*.

3. Andrew Motion, *Philip Larkin: A Writer's Life* (London: Faber, 1993), pp.13-14. The extract comes from an unfinished autobiographical essay, Notebook 5, Philip Larkin Archive, Brynmor Jones Library, University of Hull.

4. *CP*, p.33.

5. *CP*, p.152.

6. *CP*, p. 180.

7. 'Round the Point', reprinted in Philip Larkin, *Trouble at Willow Gables and Other Fictions*, ed. James Booth (London: Faber, 2002), p.479.

8. *CP*, p.126.

9. *CP*, p.175.

10. *CP*, p.215.

11. *CP*, p.67.

12. *CP*, p.165.

13. *CP*, p.29.

14. *CP*, p.33.

15. Philip Larkin: *Early Poems and Juvenilia*, ed. A.T. Tolley (London: Faber, 2005), p.62.

16. *Early Poems and Juvenilia*, p.68.

17. *CP*, p.114.

18. 'An Interview with Noel Powell', Tracks 1, 1967, reprinted in Philip Larkin, *Further Requirements* (London: Faber, 2003), pp. 31-32.

19. *Selected Letters of Philip Larkin*, ed. Anthony Thwaite (London: Faber, 1992), pp.34-35; hereinafter, *SLPL*.

20. D.H. Lawrence, *Psychoanalysis and the Unconscious; Fantasia of the Unconscious*, ed. Bruce Steele (Cambridge: Cambridge University Press, 2004).

21. Edward Mendelson, *Early Auden* (London: Faber, 1981), p.56.

22. *SLPL*, p.52.

23. *DPL*, 1.2.12, unpublished diary, Philip Larkin Archive, Brynmor Jones Library, University of Hull.

24. Philip Larkin, *Collected Poems*, ed. Anthony Thwaite (London: Faber, 2003), p.49.

25. James Booth, *Philip Larkin: The Poet's Plight* (Basingstoke: Palgrave Macmillan, 2005), p.155.

26. Philip Larkin, *Early Poems and Juvenilia*, p.157.

27. See Note 10.

28. 'Something to do with Violence', Grevel Lindop, *PN Review*, November-December 2004, Volume 32, No.2.

29. W.H. Auden, *Collected Shorter Poems, 1927-1937* (London: Faber, 1966), p.126.

30. Norman Page, *A.E Housman: A Critical Biography* (Basingstoke: Palgrave Macmillan, 1996), p.125.

31. 'Trouble at Willow Gables' and 'Michaelmas Term at St Brides',

Trouble at Willow Gables and Other Fictions.
32. Andrew Motion, *PLWL*, p.468.
33. *SLPL*, p.107.
34. See Note 3.
35. Alice Miller, *The Drama of Being a Child*, tr. Ruth Ward (London, Virago Press, 1987), p. 143.
36. Philip Larkin, *Early Poems and Juvenilia*, p.16.
37. Evelyn Waugh, *Decline and Fall* (London: Penguin Books, 2003), p.85.
38. *CP*, p.32.
39. Three psychologists in the USA set out to answer the question of how human beings stay sane and optimistic in the knowledge of personal extinction – in other words, to answer Larkin's question, 'Why aren't they screaming?' The fear of death is normally suppressed, and among the means of suppression are religion and national identity. Subjects were asked to think about their own death and then compared with controls in their subsequent performance of tasks. The following passage describes the results.
'Many of the experiments show just how pervasive is the link between reminders of death, or "mortality salience", and our reactions to people who do or do not share our particular world-view.' Holly McGregor at the University of Arizona and colleagues found that following mortality salience people were more likely to administer large quantities of chilli sauce to a chilli-hating third party who did not hold the same political views as themselves, than to someone whose politics matched their own. Likewise, Greenberg and others found that Christian subjects rated other Christians more positively than Jews after experiencing mortality salience. And researchers from the University of Mainze in Germany showed that German students sat closer to a fellow German and further away from a Turk after contemplating their own death'. (Kate Douglas, 'Death Defying', *New Scientist*, 28 August 2004)
40. The inscription on Larkin's headstone in Cottingham.

III *Line, Women and Song*

IAMBUS, king of all the North,
Sucking TROCHEES ventured forth.
DACTYLS came galloping out of the west,
But he fought and he conquered that ANAPAEST.
SPONDEE![1]

The King of the North's foot, as every poetry reader knows, consists of an unstressed syllable followed by a stressed one. Anatomically, this is relevant: footsteps, after all, proceed by a heel-toe rhythm, with the heavier, longer stress being placed on the toe-pad. The Trochee, which reverses the stress-pattern of the Iamb, is named after the Greek for 'running foot' – and the reason that King Iambus is sucking trochees is, presumably, because the anonymous author is punning on the word, *troche*, meaning lozenge, from the Greek *trokhos*, meaning 'wheel'.

Length is a consideration: the Greek and Latin authors thought in terms of syllable lengths (quantity) rather than stress. Generally, we translate from the horizontal to the vertical when we apply the old prosodic terms to English poetry. It's an imperfect method, and contemporary prosodists such as Derek Attridge have devised a more finely-tuned system of stress-measurement.[2] This has not rendered the classical system redundant as far as most traditional literary texts are concerned, though, and being of the pounds, shillings and pence generation, I shall stick mostly with the approximate but evocative ancestral glossary – evocative not only because the words themselves are etymologically resonant but because they link us to the way the poets of the past learned and thought.

There are various other kinds of foot, such as the pyrrhic (two successive unstressed syllables) but the little narrative jingle above describes, in descending order, the most common. The number of feet in the line normally ranges from one (monometer) to eight (octometer). These are the ways the poetic line traditionally orders itself, and it might be thought that its options are sadly limited. But that would be like saying the moves on a chessboard are limited. Between the stressed and the unstressed phoneme are gradations of micro-stresses and degrees of silence. Over the centuries, the English line has proceeded to absorb an inexhaustible rhythmic variety.

A poet's line is more than a matter of rhythm, or stress patterns, of course. It's a microcosm of all the varied elements, diction, register, imagery, etc. that go into the making of a whole poem. But I want to focus mainly on this bare, rather skeletal aspect of the poem's anatomy. Structured according to the principles of the metrical foot described above, the line roamed along largely unchanged for centuries until the late 19th and early 20th century when poets tried steering it in dramatic new directions. Though the process is difficult to talk about – and, after all, poetry has many easier riches to explore – the journey of the line is a fascinating one. From classical prosody to twentieth-century feminist theory, its pulsation and energy have been linked to the human body. Now that our literary culture is, generally, more receptive to women's poetic input, it might be time at least to begin examining whether rhythm and lineation are gendered territory.

What is the point of metre and rhyme – other than mnemonic? The linear suitcase helps a poet pack only the essential stuff and, by compression, achieve density and connection. And if a regular symmetrical pattern has been established, any disruption is far more noticeable and effective. Above all, lineation heightens rhythm and intensifies assonance. It produces verbal melody and harmony which affect the hearer emotionally, working at a physiological level and chiming in with, or perhaps even re-setting, our bodily rhythms. While poetry's appeal is less visceral than that of music (the instant availability of music at its most immediately visceral, rock and pop and the 'light' classics, is I believe a major reason for the decline of poetry's audience) its phonic pulsations heighten, as they result from, the fundamental human delight in language, our sense of an organic correspondence with it. Our most intimate connection with language is through poetry, because it allows such a dense interplay of verbal responses.

Footstep or heartbeat, the staple metre of English verse is

the iambic pentameter. There is so much poetry written in that metre that it's hard to select a single example, something you might give to new creative writing students, for instance. But why not take the first line of John Clare's poem, 'I am?': 'I am – yet what I am none cares or knows'.[3] It contains a useful mnemonic for the beginner: 'I am' is in fact an Iamb. And it shows us, interestingly, that length of syllable does vary in English. 'Am' in both cases is a stressed syllable, but the first 'am' surely lingers for longer on the lips than the second. Attridge's distinction between stress and secondary stress is relevant. The second 'am' takes a stress, but a weaker one.

Why does the first stressed beat sing out so strongly? I think it is partly a matter of the syntax, or the rhetoric of the syntax. First, the ear expects the more usual, copular usage of the verb 'to be', e.g. 'I am happy', 'I am a man'. There is a tiny shock in registering that the phrase is meant existentially, and thus grammatically complete. Then the statement is followed by qualification, as if the disruptive little conjunction 'yet' overturned its claim to authority. Important, too, is the dash after the first 'am'. It emphasises the pause already there, and ensures we give it a slightly bigger measure of resonant space. But mainly it is the way we speak, the natural rhythm of English, that is directing the stress variations.

An actor reading that line would probably go for an even more exaggerated pause than the reader mentally reciting it. But however long you pause after the first 'I am' you don't alter the number of stresses or beats in the line. You may pause for as long as you like, but only when you continue 'yet what I am none cares or knows' does the mental pulse-check resume.

The tenacity of the iambic pentameter in the broad landscape of English poetry seems extraordinary. From the Tabard Inn, Southwark, to the Royal Station Hotel, Hull, the seven centuries might be a mere hop. 'Bifil that in that seson on a day, / In Southwerk at the Tabard as I lay, / Redy to wenden on my pilgrymage / To Caunterbury with ful devout corage, / At nyght was come into that hostelrye / Wel nyne and twenty in a compaignye, / Of sondry folk…' Thus Chaucer sets the scene for the introduction of his fellow pilgrims in the 'General Prologue' to *The Canterbury Tales*.[4] Larkin's sonnet 'Friday Night in the Royal

Station Hotel' begins with two trochaic lines: 'Light spreads darkly downwards from the high / Clusters of lights over empty chairs/ That face each other, coloured differently. / Through open doors, the dining-room declares / A larger loneliness of knives and glass / And silence laid like carpet...' [5] Ignoring the effects of contrasted rhyme-scheme, and listening simply to the pulse of the line, the differences are slight. Chaucer's line is pleasingly flexible (with a trochaic line 3). Larkin's use of the metre is only a little less regular, most noticeably in the second line where a silent beat is inserted: 'Clusters of lights (beat) over empty chairs'. Here, in fact, Larkin creates an invisible rest-mark, having set up a metrical expectation that our ear does not willingly disrupt.

Chaucer would not have broken the line between an adjective and a noun ('high / Clusters') and this is the point where we first register, rhythmically, the sharp presence of the 20th century. Middle English had a more flexible word-order at its disposal than Modern. Hear it in the very first line of the 'General Prologue': 'Whan that Aprill with his shoures soote'. It would be peculiar for a 20th-century poet to place a single adjective after the noun in such a construction. Our poetic convention requires the line to fit in with current speech habits: though the convention of course will be challenged and changed one day, if our speech patterns change or if a new Ezra Pound (let's call her Suzi Cent) decides that poetry after all requires a separate elevated language. What appears to have happened between Chaucer's time and Larkin's is that word order rigidified in the English sentence, and the poetic line was permitted certain compensatory informalities regarding the line-break.

Besides accentual-syllabic metre (i.e. the metre that takes into account both stressed and unstressed syllables, and where the groups of syllables conform to the normal speech stress), there are two other significant metrical systems – accentual metre and syllabics. In accentual metre only the stress is counted: you can hear it in Anglo-Saxon alliterative verse, in many nursery rhymes and in contemporary 'rap'. There is an identical number of stresses in each line, no set number of syllables, and no arrangement between stressed and unstressed syllables. In syllabic poetry, syllables only are counted and stress, ostensibly, is ignored.

The number of syllables per line, varied or regular, probably registers subliminally with the reader even if not counted consciously. The form becomes almost visual in the poetry of Marianne Moore because she uses varied-length lines (quantitative syllabics) in a repeated stanza-pattern, and we can see fairly easily what is afoot (or not). Her rhyme-schemes also, perhaps, help to place us in the numerical pattern, as in the 1,3,9,6,8-syllable design of 'The Fish:' [6]

> wade
> through black jade.
>> Of the crow-blue mussel-shells, one keeps
>> adjusting the ash-heaps;
>>> opening and shutting itself like
>
> an
> injured fan... (etc.)

Words are not easily subdued to a syllabic tick-tock. Their different phonetic quantities and stress patterns are never escaped. Moore's lines have a lively accentual rhythm, and her one-syllable line at the start of each stanza even gives a normally unstressed word like the indefinite article, 'an', a syncopation-like stress. A syllabic poem will often sound as if it's weaving between metrically patterned lines and lines that have become interestingly distressed, despite adhering strictly to the syllabic count it has established.

The five-syllable lines of Sylvia Plath's 'Mushrooms',[7] for example, often ask to be heard as dactyl-trochee patterns: 'soft fists insist on / heaving the needles', 'perfectly voiceless / widen the crannies' but the syllabic grid ensures that such glimmers of metrical regularity never pall into monotony. Practically every tercet has a line or lines in which the stresses fall quite differently, as in the opening stanza ('Overnight, very / Whitely, discreetly, / Very quietly...'), where two monometric lines frame the dactylic and dimetric second.

The basic art of prosody is the art of working with and against an implied regularity. Syntax, the flow of the sentence over the line, is the most obvious way of creating counter-currents. It may be a dramatic, sharply articulated movement, as in the Marianne Moore example, or barely noticeable, as in the first stanza of Tennyson's 'In Memoriam A.H.H.:' [8]

> I held it truth, with him who sings
> To one clear harp in divers tones,
> That men may rise on stepping-stones
> Of their dead selves to higher things.

The single sentence here pours like a waterfall over the line-breaks. The end of the adverbial clause coincides with the end of the second line, but because the reader's ear and mind are waiting for the subject of 'I held it truth' there is little sense of an end-stop, and our attention is held uninterruptedly. Of course, grammatically, there could be a full-stop at the end of line 3. But Tennyson makes a daring enjambement, carrying the genitive construction, 'The stepping stones of their dead selves', across the line-break in a way that, after first administering a tiny shock, feels inevitable. Metre and rhyme are strictly regular, but their force is subdued.

What happens to the line when it is lengthened far beyond the usual metric boundaries, yet still firmly belongs to poetic metre? Perhaps in response to the new stream-of-consciousness techniques being explored by the prose-writers of her time, Charlotte Mew (*b.* 1867) produced poems of such long lines that she requested the printers of her first book, *The Farmer's Bride* to typeset it sideways.

'On the Road to the Sea' [9] is a good example of her discursive style of dramatic monologue:

> We passed each other, turned and stopped for half an hour, then
> went our way.
> I who make other women smile did not make you –
> But no man can move mountains in a day.
> So this hard thing is yet to do.

That first long line actually smuggles two iambic tetrameters in its portmanteau: 'We passed each other, turned and stopped, / For half an hour, then went our way.'

Separated in this way, the segments add up to no more than a dull little jingle – but, merged, they form into a fluent, ambulatory, strangely seductive opening line. By softening the end-of-line pause (it seems particularly unobtrusive, as if it fell simply where the line or its speaker needed to take a breath) Mew almost escapes her own metrical ear and all the monologue's lines, even the short emphatic ones, convey the casual, slightly prosy rhythm that the genre requires. At the same time, the speech rhythms are landscaped into quite familiar metrical patterns. The second line, for instance, is an Alexandrine, a 12-syllable line Mew was fond of and which testifies to the importance of French influences in her work. The third is iambic pentameter and the fourth iambic tetrameter, this time un-doubled.

The first stanza does not form a template for the rest of the poem. Each stanza is metrically distinct. Their length varies between four and eight lines. Mew further complicates the issue by indenting some of the lines. Then, in stanza four, she introduces a Dickinson-like use of dashes – in fact, she complicates the pauses by adding a semi-colon after each dash, and a pair of brackets mid-way!

> Today is not enough or yesterday. God sees it all –
> Your length on sunny lawns, the wakeful rainy nights – ; tell me – ;
> (how vain to ask) but it is not a question – just a call – ;
> Show me then, only your notched inches climbing up the garden wall,
> I like you best when you are small.

The quadruple rhyme, the magnificent, hesitating length of the second line (based on three iambic trimeters followed by an iambic pentameter) and the shyly cadenced tetrameter of the last line have the effect of a shadow lengthening and shrinking. This strangely unsettled poem, a monologue that is also a dialogue, is torn between stability and instability, withdrawal and predation ('But first I want your life'), hope and fear. The speaker appears to be a young man who has just enlisted and who 'may not be here / tonight, tomorrow morning or next year'. He has no hope of possessing the young woman, and his thoughts have some quality of entranced, unbounded fantasy. He resembles Death in the archetypal encounter of Death and the Maiden, especially in the last three menacingly tender lines: 'Still I will let you keep your life a little while, / See dear? / *I have made you smile.*' The second of those lines, ('see dear'), is a spondee, the two-stressed foot that means in Greek *libation*: the pouring of an offering to the gods, of wine or oil or blood. The extraordinary lineation and punctuation throughout 'The Road to the Sea' make us feel the ebb and flow of remembered emotion and speech; it's as if a pen were constantly moving over the page of a diary.

It is more difficult to achieve this counterpoint of syntax and linear grid in free-verse. The American poet and scholar, John Hollander, demonstrates the problem in his compendium of prosodic examples, *Rhyme's Reason: A Guide to English Verse*: [10]

> Free verse is never totally free.
> It can occur in many forms,
> All of them having in common one principle –
> Nothing is necessarily counted or measured...
> One form – this one – makes each line a grammatical unit...

E.J. Thribbishly, Hollander concludes 'such verse often tends / To fall very flat'.

The technique has its uses, and can, for example, be effective in the short poem aiming at an intense, imagistic focus. But more frequently rhythmical dullness results from the lack of argument between syntax and line.

Another free-verse technique Hollander describes uses plentiful enjambement. It is the default setting of much contemporary poetry, and is capable of numerous varied effects and charges of energy. Again, Hollander demonstrates the technique by using it: 'Free verse can, like a shrewd smuggler, contain more / Measured kinds of line, hidden/ Inside its own more random-seeming/ Ones...' In a vivid simile he explains that it's 'a little/ like putting a contour map/ over a street-plan'.

Adrienne Rich began her career as a formalist, and though she re-made her prosody and her line, accentual syllabic patterns are still an audible base in some of her free-verse writing. Rich is a complex poet, a genuinely public writer who can talk persuasively for others, and, in more personal vein, carefully interrogates her own perceptions and assumptions. Her lines move with a quiet authority that draws on this underlying metrical sense. In the second stanza of 'Yom Kippur, 1984',[11] an extended meditation on the question of her Jewish identity, she smuggles in a homage to Walt Whitman as well as a metrical echo:

> Three thousand miles from what I once called home
> I open a book searching for some lines I remember
> about flowers, something to bind me to this coast as lilacs in the
>   dooryard once
> bound me back there – yes, lupines on a burnt mountainside,
> something that bloomed and faded and was written down
> in the poet's book, forever:

That is the contour map: under it lies the street-plan. Those same lines can be arranged so as to bring up a sound-track of loose-limbed iambic pentameter:

> Three thousand miles from what I once called home,
> I open a book searching for some lines
> I remember about flowers, something to bind me
> To this coast as lilacs in the dooryard bound me
> Back there – yes, lupines on a burnt
> Mountainside, something that bloomed and faded
> And was written down in the poet's book forever...

The symmetrical pattern registers, however faintly, because the first line is our old friend, iambic pentameter, called up to heighten the mood which is the ancient sadness of exile. However, Rich does not want such easy effects. She quickly erases the metrical echo, and line 3 cannot be read as we read Mew's long lines. There is no sense of a metrical topography. The line is pure prose rhythm, or thinking-aloud rhythm. Its contour rambles almost off the map.

We haven't so far paid much attention to varieties of silence – or what is popularly called 'the white space' around the poem. But, first, what of the white space within the line? It's easy to forget the obvious, that the spaces between the words are un-sounded. Unless a metrical expectation has been established (see the Larkin line quoted earlier) any desired caesura must be deliberately created, by punctuation or additional spacing. Otherwise, separate signifiers run into a single unit of melody until the end of the line.

Many recent and contemporary poets have tried to give silence a larger role in the poem's line or stanza, using such devices as extra spacing within the line   like this or
                                                  the stepped caesura.
Mina Loy (*b*. 1882) pre-dates E.E. Cummings (*b*. 1894) as a pioneer of irregular spacing (the Anglo-Saxon poets had of course used a regularly falling medial caesura) and it's a technique that has by no means exhausted its potential. Adrienne Rich is a skilful exponent. Denise Riley takes the device a stage further in her poem, 'Affections must not', by combining double-spacing and full-stops. Thus a one-sentence trimetric line, 'I neglect the house', is elongated into 'I. neglect. the. house', a satisfying synthesis of combative lethargy.[12]

The rhythms of most contemporary poetry remain extremely close to speech-rhythms. It's easier to escape the tyranny of meaning than the tyranny of stress. Inevitably, the ear wants to part-scan the free-est poetic line because even random patterns of stressed and unstressed syllables contain metrical shadows, ghosts of accentual syllabic metres which bring to mind Hollander's contour map over a street-plan. The spacing used by Denise Riley above effectively held speech rhythm at bay, forcing readers to recite the line more slowly than in average speechtime and to stress all the words. Alice Oswald uses the opposite technique in the first poem of her latest collection, *Woods etc.*

'Sea Poem'[13] opens with a question that could be read as trochaic pentameter, followed by an answering line that calls such symmetry into question, as if the water were describing itself: 'what is water in the eyes of water / loose inquisitive fragile anxious / a wave, a winged form / splitting up into sharp glances'. That four-word second line demonstrates the rhythmic mimesis that poetry's new foot-loose flexibility can achieve so beautifully. The absence of commas between the adjectives accelerates our pronunciation and minimises the stress. Assonantally, there is a little heave between the sibilants, making a small wave-like sound. What happens then is that, although the lines might seem to restore a metrical count, we read them less emphatically. One line always tries to tell us how to read the next one: that's how poetry works.

Like a number of contemporary British poets, Oswald frequently uses regular stanza structures. Stanzas provide a kind of visual reassurance (this is poetry, we still have symmetry) – perhaps this is why quatrains are enduringly popular. They also allow poets to play with degrees of closure. Though lines are frequently enjambed over the stanza break, the stanza break is never insignificant: the effect is similar to that of a note tied over the bar-line in music. Could it be that the stanza is beginning to take the place of the line as the primary poetic unit?

Ruth Padel, a poet who emerged relatively recently with such collections as *Rembrandt Would Have Loved You*, *Voodoo Shop* and *The Soho Leopard*, is one of those writers who seems to think in terms of the shape and energy of the stanza. Her poems often use a big stanza-structure, with a variable metre that comes close to the accentual, now pulling the line almost as long as it will go, now letting it snap back small. Her lineation owes something to Hopkins and sprung rhythm – and, she says, to Greek drama, 'particularly choral lyrics in tragedy. The way the words curl in images over each other, the way a song is built up through images, and the delicate language, acidly sensuous but probing moral questions of belief and fear and the fragility of life all the time. The way one word can turn the whole feel of a poem over on itself – I learnt that all from the Greek poets. The lyric poets, Sappho, Alcaeus, Pindar, but mainly the tragic poets and Homer. Structure, movement through and images.' [14]

Padel uses a good deal of enjambement, but breaks the line so that we hear the stress of the last word resonating through the beginning word of the new line. Here's the first stanza of 'Writing to Onegin', [15] a poem which is not so much a translation as a dance: it dances with Pushkin's images and narrative to a beat that is entirely Padel's:

> Look at the bare wood hand-waxed floor and long
> White dressing-gown, the good child's writing-desk
>   And passionate cold feet
> Summoning music of the night, timbrels, gongs
> And gamelans. And one neat pen, one candle
>   Puckering its life out hour by hour. Is 'Tell
> Him I love him' never a good idea? You can't
> Wish this unlived – this world on fire, on storm
>   Alert, till a shepherd's song
> Outside, some hyperactive yellowhammer, bulbul,
> Wren, amplified in hills and woods, tells her to bestow
>   A spot of notice on the dawn.

Perhaps the emphasis on the stanza for some writers is a result of the amount of material that their poetry wants to convey. Poetry trawls a busy culture, absorbing and retransmitting a montage of sense impressions and sound-bites. But the stanza still consists of lines and the art of building it depends on that linear distribution of energy and emphasis.

The American critic Helen Vendler describes lineation as an enactment of narrative or emotional meaning. 'A "good" line-break in a poem always reflects a change of direction – an alteration in tone, a veering of glance, a shift in metaphor...' [16] The notion of the 'good line-break' is of course a reflection of 20th century practice. In non-metrical writing, dealing with the line-break is a major skill, and the concept of 'good', i.e. meaningful, may vary within a poem and from poem to poem. What normally occurs at the end of the line is a silent beat. This silence dramatises and exposes the line's last word. Whether or not its megalomania is reinforced with rhyme and metre, the last word would always like to have the last word. Robert Frost made the often-quoted assertion that 'writing free verse is like playing tennis with the net down',[17] but all verse has to be played across a net, free verse no less than metrical. There is, in effect, a tennis-net at the end of each line. The poet's skill is to keep the rhythmic ball skimming over these dangerous little barriers, without entirely denying the reason for their existence, and knowing when to let the ball drop gracefully against the mesh.

Vendler's description of lineation is useful but by now slightly dated. A popular contemporary technique plays down the drama of the line-break and the line. I call work of this kind stress-limited poetry. It's still accented but the accents are rhythmically suppressed. If stress-heavy poetry, accentual and accentual-syllabic, belongs to the high street chain, stress-limited poetry is designer-boutique stuff. It's more fashionable and more difficult to handle. And it's more American.

It's time to say something about the American influence, because its effect on English poetry and the English language is significant and accelerating. American rhythm has entered British and Irish poetry not only via the great 19th- and 20th-century literary revisionists (Whitman, Pound, Williams *et al*), nor the contemporary work that the UK poetry presses are increasingly publishing and distributing in Britain, but, I surmise, as an unfiltered effect of the language itself. Through the mass media we tune constantly into varieties of spoken American and the dominant tone, I think, has entered the shared linguistic blood-stream, inculcating a flatter stress-pattern.

We can hear it in some of the earlier poetry, too. Listen to William Carlos Williams, who set out his explanation of the 'variable foot' in a letter to Richard Eberhart,[18] quoting the opening of his poem 'To Daphne and Virginia',[19] and numbering the segments from one to six, thus:

(1) The smell of the heat is boxwood
    (2) when rousing us
        (3) a movement of the air
(4) stirs our thoughts
    (5) that had no life in them
        (6) to a life, a life in which...

'Count a different beat to each numeral' Williams instructed Eberhart. This, as will immediately be apparent, is difficult for an English native-speaker to do. My own ear wants to make three metrical feet out of 'the smell of the heat is boxwood', hearing it as iambic trimeter, with an additional short syllable in the second foot creating an anapaest, 'of the heat' and a feminine ending to the third ('is boxwood'). But if I lightly Americanise my accent, I can say it quite easily as a one-beat unit. It means speaking quicker, eliding more of the syllables, blurring the sharp little consonant 't' in 'heat' so it sounds faintly like 'th'. 'Thesmelloftheheatisboxwood'. Not a heart-beat or footstep of King Iambus remains, but a brief, carefree pioneering dance, with a single mild stress, falling on 'smell'.

Williams's 'variable foot' is really a variety of accentual metre. There is no extended metrical pattern, but each short line-segment is compressed into a kind of foot, and each foot is given its own line, or segment of line. Paradoxically, Williams actually ends up creating emphatic-sounding poetry. His linear units are frequently self-contained, making maximal, rather percussive use of the white spaces around them. Within the line, though, the stresses are minimal.

What I call the stress-limited technique is frequently used by younger British poets. Henry Shukman's 'Sunday'[20] begins:

Let's talk about Sunday, how we drove
across a simple land, land of an easier time,
past fogbound trees, among alloyed affluence.
Neither of us knew how much hope
the other held, but we'd been listening
to Miles Davis, he set an easy Sunday tone.

As in Padel's verse-structures, enjambement seems to be the key device, but here it subdues the line-end drama to recreate the 'easy Sunday tone', the laid-back jazz style. The line-breaks are plain on the page but less easy to hear. The poet seems to have arranged for them to occur at points where they will be least audible, most grammatically embedded. At the same time, there is a sense of diffused anxiety. The lines seem to be looking for an elusive point of rest.

Not all the lines are enjambed, but, overall, the stress-signals are faint and depend on pronunciation (there is no regulatory metre to tell us how to pronounce them). Emphasis is spread over the syllable groups. This is true of the beginnings of the lines, too. 'Across a simple land' seems to demand one stress, as does 'neither of us knew'. As with Willams's 'variable foot', to clarify these phrases in metrical terms we would have to slow down the line to an un-natural degree and introduce an artificial-sounding accent which would spoil the effect. The poet's purpose seems to be to retain as much of a low-key speech-like rhythm as possible –'Let's talk about Sunday'- while maintaining a faint syncopating under-pulse of accentual-syllabic tension.

Poetry used to orate: now it murmurs and chatters. Behind writers like Shukman stand the great American conversational poets such as Frank O'Hara and John Ashbery, whose work, even on the page, recreates such an uncannily individual speaking tone. And behind them stand Williams, Olson and Pound, with their various theories of poetry as speech-based and American-speaking. Numberless English-language poets are currently working in a manner similar to the Projective Verse style outlined by Olson: they approach the new poem as if it were an open area, a field, and work with the energy of the voice.[21]

The politics that underlay the modernist revolt against form has by now been absorbed into poetry's unconscious. But there is a lingering polarisation – for example in the way we speak of "closed" versus "open" forms, and discriminate between "mainstream" and "avant garde", attributing greater democratic credentials to the latter, despite the fact that avant garde poetry is often heavily theorised and makes little attempt to charm or teach an ordinary reader. The accentual-syllabic line is associated with an oratory which no longer convinces us, but the voice of the elite has simply migrated into a poetry based on theory. Women's writing can also be divided in this way – and according to some (I think confused) critical orthodoxies, reaction against traditional form would seem an essential element in the construction of a feminist poetics.

Poets as different as Edith Sitwell and Eavan Boland have gendered traditional form as male. But if we view, say, the sonnet as an inherently masculine form, what do we make of its highly successful practice by such writers as Christina Rossetti, Elizabeth Barrett Browning, Augusta Webster or the underrated Edna St Vincent Millay? The sonnet, an Italian import, is clearly more suited to an inflected language rich in rhyme sounds, and more manageable in an English syntax permitting flexible word-order. A classical education no doubt helped earlier writers. The flowering of the form in English coincided historically with a period of great imperial expansion, and many sonnets were composed by men of influence and leisure. But the form's development depended on freelances like Shakespeare, and, later, peasants like Clare. Some outsiders interestingly realigned its inner balances. After all, a sonnet is not symmetrically rigid like a table. Nor is it inherently a little model of empire: it's very structure invites a "turn", a self-interrogation. It is an organic, breathing thing, made of language, pliable. It depends on outsiders and interrogators and other kinds of maverick to keep it alive.

Women's absence from the canon and past curricula must have greatly aided the view that form was itself discriminatory. As literary history goes on being revised by the proliferation of period anthologies of their writing, we can see women handling rhyme and metre with perfect skill and sincerity, even as they make their ironical little bows to the patriarchal conventions that say their brains are not really up to poetry.

Fluency in strict form depends on immersion in formal verse and a good ear. I wonder how many poets may in fact be oppressed by the anti-formalist demand that in order to make things new they should work against a natural grain? Anne Stevenson recalls Elizabeth Bishop's telling her that 'unlike Marianne Moore, she was really an umpty-tumpty poet'.[22] Happily for us, Bishop resisted that inclination – yet she needed the inclination as a basis for her more flexible rhythms. Perhaps 20th-century poetry is the story of umpty-tumpty poets finding ingenious ways not to be. The 21st century story may be of poets who have genuinely forgotten what 'umpty-tumpty' sounds like.

Supposing form were inherently, hormonally, muscularly,

temperamentally male (as I can't help feeling rugby football, Sumo wrestling and some other competitive sports may be), wouldn't we currently have more male players? The number of poets, male and female, writing formal verse is fairly small and probably dwindling. There is no way of knowing if the free-form male poets have been influenced by feminist politics, the general zeitgeist, or the presence of female hormones in our water supply, but I rather suspect the zeitgeist, working in areas of absorption never particularly subject to gender-distinction.

Testing the hunch that as few male as female poets currently favoured structures using symmetry and rhyme, I took *The Forward Book of Poetry, 2004*, as a sample. The anthology is published annually and consists of poems selected from books and magazines published in the UK and Ireland, assembled under various categories ('Best Single Poem', 'Best First Collection', etc). One anthology and a small-ish selection of one year's work can't tell the whole story of contemporary poetry in these islands (especially as work by Americans is included) but as a repre-sentative selection of recnt UK-published material it must tell us something. I chose the 2004 edition from no ulterior motive and for no better reason than it was the most up-to-date one I had to hand.[23]

There were 52 poets in the 2004 edition, 24 women and 28 men. The selectors, incidentally, were four women with a male "chair". I found that 21 out of the 67 poems had a regular or fairly regular metre and rhyme-scheme, and, of those, six were by women. There were another 6 poems whose lines were mainly what I call stress-limited (many more used some degree of stress limitation within an accentual syllabic framework), and five of these were by women. There were three sonnets in the collec-tion – all by male poets! On the evidence of this sample, men were more likely to favour form.

Forty-six poems avoided rhyme-schemes, but metrical under-tones were clearly audible in most. And the majority, at least two-thirds, favoured some kind of regular or near-regular stanzaic organisation. The difference between male and female practice is certainly worth noting. More male than female poets wrote metrically, and more female poets played down the stresses of the line. But the majority of men and women wrote similarly, in rhythmic structures that were essentially a compromise, operating between the metrical and stress-limited extremes.

Enough women have written, and are still writing, accentual-syllabic poetry to suggest that it is not intrinsically, neurologically, against the grain. For many contemporary poets (Carol Ann Duffy, Jackie Kay, Anne Stevenson, Fleur Adcock) it is a resource, not a habit. Marilyn Hacker is an interesting exception. Like Adrienne Rich, she is Jewish, Lesbian and libertarian. She too plots in her private corner of the public restaurant a sharp protest at social injustice, and envisages new communities and womanly networks. In a very different manner, she is concerned with unveiling society's 'lies, secrets, silence'. But her poetry is formal. It demonstrates the lasting versatility of traditional metre, showing that it can embrace conversational idioms and the rush of contemporary experience without severe distortion or artifice.

In the sonnet, '1973',[24] the metrical line is intercut with everyday speech-rhythms: '"I'm pregnant," I wrote to her in delight / from London, thirty, married, in print. A fools- / cap sheet scrawled slantwise with one minuscule / sentence came back. "I hope your child is white".' The line-breaks facilitate the rhyme-scheme, but that isn't their purpose: they dramatise the difficulty between the two women, and the speaker's shock and disgust. The poem follows its first reluctant turn towards resolution with another, more dramatic turn.

> I grudgingly acknowledged her 'good hair,'
> which wasn't, very, from my point of view.
> 'No tar-brush left,' her father's mother said.
> 'She's Jewish and she's white', from her cranked bed
> mine smugly snapped.
>   She's Black. She is a Jew.

The stunning force of the last line is achieved by the stepped caesura, followed by two short statements, both strong but differently weighted. The accent falls exactly on the final 'is' which is also the point of the conversational (and intellectual and moral) emphasis. Hacker's work ought to convince anyone still in doubt that "closed form" does not equal "closed mind" – nor does it mean that there are no secret doors *within* the form, waiting to be unlocked. She is heir to the Elizabeth Bishop of 'One Art',[25] taking a form to the limits of disturbance, and using its boundaries to dramatise the inner cross-currents.

My concern over the decay of rhyme and accentual-syllabic metre (and the wonderful rhetorical devices that spring from compressions) is that poetry will lose its musicality. How odd that Pound and Eliot considered poetry most musical when it avoided metre. At this historical juncture, our a-metrical poetry sounds much more like spoken prose than music. The musical phrase seems to need some resonance from the metrical grid in order to emerge.

Pound also believed that 'a vast number of subjects cannot be precisely, and therefore not properly, rendered in symmetrical forms'.[26] Again, I think he was wrong: if the subjects can be talked about in the English language they can be expressed in the poetic forms of the English language. It's possible, though, that metre and form, whatever discord you allow within them, will tend to usher a poem towards a state of resolution, and I concede that this is not always desirable. You might want a poem to exit muttering to itself. But there has to be some resolution – a poem is not a slice of life.

Poetry needs to maintain integrity as a genre. From the reader's point of view, it also needs to be capable of being described. One of the reasons for our poor receptivity (including our inadequate critical discourse, so often more interested in theory on the one hand and the personality of the poet on the other) is that contemporary poetry is a plethora of nonce-forms that no one has 'world enough and time' to itemise. Misapplied political tact compounds the problem, and critical evaluation has become almost taboo.[27]

The business of the poet changes according to his or her society, and the contract must be agreed between them. Poetry has narrated the history of the people, praised princes and gods, sung armies to war, proclaimed the news and the new. Today it has a number of minor roles, often market-driven and second-hand. It can "heal your soul" or make you laugh or reinforce your ethnic identity. It is an arm of literary theory or linguistic philosophy. It sells you cat-food or non-conformity, opposing the tainted simplicities of consumerism (while on sale in all good bookshops) with self-cancelling multiplicities of meaning.

I am all for poetry as a force of opposition – and as a form of linguistic play. A poem will tend to be both those things, *qua* poem. But I think that primarily it is a truthfully-conducted invitation to explore someone else's humanity. Ordering its insights into a pleasure-giving pattern (because it is an art-form, after all) a poem can only finally show us, through language, a human being being human. It gives us his or her self – idiolect, mood, odour, texture, rhythm – embodied in lexicon.

Can we make new 21st century rhythms? We should certainly try out more sculptural and inventive approaches to the line – but we mustn't forget, either, that innovation, in an art of minute detail, may itself exist in the finest of verbal shadings. Denise Levertov, pairing Black Mountain rhythms with a kind of biblical English reminds us, finally, that there are times for poetry to sing, times for a good tune and a firm beat. SPONDEE!

> Stand fast in thy place:
> remember Caedmon
> turning from song was met
> in his cow-barn by One who set him
> to sing the beginning.
> Live
> in thy fingertips and in thy
> hair's rising; hunger
> be thine, food
> be thine and what wine
> will not shrivel thee.
> Breathe deep of
> evening, be with the
> rivers of tumult, sharpen
> thy wits to know power and be
> humble.[27]

NOTES

1. Theodore Bernstein, 'The Careful Writer', quoted by Jim Coats on AWADmail Issue 133, 28.08.04, Wordsmith.org.

2. Derek Attridge, *Poetic Rhythm: An Introduction* (Cambridge: Cambridge University Press, 1995).

3. John Clare: *Major Works*, ed. Eric Robinson & David Powell (Oxford: OUP, 1984), p.361.

4. Geoffrey Chaucer, *The Canterbury Tales*. A useful website, with notes and glossary, is http://www.librarius.com/cantales.htm

5. Philip Larkin, *Collected Poems* (London: Faber, 2003), p.130.

6. Marianne Moore, *The Complete Poems* (London: Faber, 1972).

7. Sylvia Plath, *Collected Poems* (London: Faber and Faber, 1981), p.139.

8. See the complete text in, for example, *Victorian Poetry: An Annotated Anthology*, ed. Francis O'Gorman (Oxford: Blackwell Publishing, 2004).

9. Charlotte Mew, *Collected Poems and Prose*, ed. Val Warner (Manchester: Carcanet, 1981), p.29. See also the Introduction for Warner's comments on Mew's long lines, pp. xvii–xviii.

10. John Hollander, *Rhyme's Reason: A Guide to English Verse* (New Haven: Yale University Press, 1981).

11. Adrienne Rich, *Your Native Land, Your Life* (New York: W.W. Norton, 1986).

12. Denise Riley, *Dry Air* (London: Virago Press, 1985).

13. Alice Oswald, *Woods etc.* (London: Faber, 2005).

14. Ruth Padel, 'How and Why', *Contemporary Women's Poetry*, ed. Alison Mark & Deryn Rees-Jones, (Basingstoke: Macmillan Press, 2000), p.15.

15. Ruth Padel, *Voodoo Shop* (London, Chatto & Windus, 2002).

16. Helen Vendler, 'The Three Acts of Criticism', *London Review of Books*, 26 May 1994.

17. Robert Frost, an 'Address' given at the Milton Academy, Milton, Mass., 17 May 1935.

18. William Carlos Williams, 'A New Measure', *Modern Poets on Modern Poetry*, ed. James Scully (London & Glasgow, Collins Fontana, 1971), pp.71–72 (quoting from a letter written to Richard Eberhart, 23 May 1954).

19. William Carlos Williams, *Selected Poems*, ed. Charles Tomlinson (London: Penguin Books, 2000), p.177.

20. Henry Shukman, *In Doctor No's Garden* (London: Jonathan Cape, 2002).

21. Charles Olson, 'Projective Verse', *Modern Poets on Modern Poetry*, pp.271–82; also in *Strong Words: Modern Poets on Modern Poetry*, ed. W.N. Herbert & Matthew Hollis (Tarset: Bloodaxe Books, 2000), pp.92–99.

22. 'A Chev'ril Glove', Anne Stevenson, *The Poet's Voice and Craft*, ed. C.B. McCully (Manchester: Carcanet, 1994), p.124.

23. *The Forward Book of Poetry 2004* (London: Forward and Faber, 2003).

24. Marilyn Hacker, '1973', *Assumptions* (New York: W.W. Norton, 1985).

25. Elizabeth Bishop, *Complete Poems* (London: Chatto & Windus, 1983).

26. Ezra Pound, 'A Retrospect', *Modern Poets on Modern Poetry*, p.37; *Strong Words*, pp.17–25.

27. For example, see Jane Dowson ('Older Sisters are Very Sobering Things', *Feminist Review*, No. 62, Summer 1999). My request for 'consolidation, stringency, sifting' of women's poetry was interpreted as meaning 'there are too many women around'. The idea that every decade or two a completely new generation of wonderful new poets springs up is market-driven fantasy. Poets need time for development. Informed commentary and constructive criticism are part of that process.

27. Denise Levertov, 'Three Meditations', *New Selected Poems* (Tarset: Bloodaxe Books, 2003), p.22.

Elizabeth Bishop: Poet of the Periphery

edited by LINDA ANDERSON & JO SHAPCOTT

Elizabeth Bishop is one of the greatest poets of the 20th century. When she died in 1979, she had only published four collections, yet had won virtually every major American literary award, including the Pulitzer Prize. She maintained close friendships with poets such as Marianne Moore and Robert Lowell, and her work has always been highly regarded by other writers. In surveys of British poets carried out in 1984 and 1994 she emerged as a surprising major choice or influence for many, from Andrew Motion and Craig Raine to Kathleen Jamie and Lavinia Greenlaw.

A virtual orphan from an early age, Elizabeth Bishop was brought up by relatives in New England and Nova Scotia. The tragic circumstances of her life – from alcoholism to repeated experiences of loss in her relationships with women – nourished an outsider's poetry notable both for its reticence and tentativeness. She once described a feeling that 'everything is interstitial' and reminds us in her poetry – in a way that is both radical and subdued – that understanding is at best provisional and that most vision is peripheral.

Since her death, a definitive edition of Bishop's *Complete Poems* (1983) has been published, along with *The Collected Prose* (1984), her letters in *One Art* (1994), her paintings in *Exchanging Hats* (1996) and Brett C. Millier's important biography (1993). In America, there have been numerous critical studies and books of academic essays, but in Britain only studies by Victoria Harrison (1995) and Anne Stevenson (1998/2006) have done anything to raise Bishop's critical profile.

Elizabeth Bishop: Poet of the Periphery is the first collection of essays on Bishop to be published in Britain, and draws on work presented at the first UK Elizabeth Bishop conference, held at Newcastle University. It brings together papers by both academic critics and leading poets, including Michael Donaghy, Vicki Feaver, Jamie McKendrick, Deryn Rees-Jones and Anne Stevenson. Academic contributors include Professor Barbara Page of Vassar College.

Newcastle/Bloodaxe Poetry Series: 1
Paperback   ISBN 1 85224 556 6   208 pages   £12

Poems 1968-2004

by CAROL RUMENS

Carol Rumens has always confronted the personal with the political in poems which are remarkable for their imaginative daring and their engagement with other lives. Often set against the background of Eastern Europe, Russia or Northern Ireland, they are filled with a powerful sense of loss and exile. She draws on a wide variety of characters and voices to dramatise the realities of suffering and persecution, or to write direct, honest accounts of love, separation, death and displacement.

'Carol Rumens is one of the few women poets writing today whose seriousness is absolute but not closed; whose political beliefs are so enmeshed with her intelligence and sympathetic passions that it is impossible to consider the state of contemporary poetry in Britain without taking her work into account...She retains her feminine voice, but extends her sympathies beyond feminism in sinewy but heart-piercing poems' – ANNE STEVENSON

'She is a European poet whose imagination goes beyond the confines of Europe, a poet of borders and transit, and of the movement across frontiers which makes both the experience of alienation and that of "home" a relative matter' – ISOBEL ARMSTRONG, *TLS*

'Her poetry achieves levels of genuine anger, expressing through gritted teeth an avowed intention to redeem, in art and love, the contemporary world that helped create them, against which they pitch themselves' – JOHN SEARS, *PopMatters*

Paperback   ISBN 1 85224 680 8   472 pages   £12

For a complete catalogue of Bloodaxe titles, please write to:
Bloodaxe Books Ltd, Highgreen, Tarset, Northumberland NE48 1RP